On a Clear Day
You Can See Yourself

On a Clear Day You Can See Yourself

·

Turning the Life You Have
Into the Life You Want

· · · · · · · · · · · · · · · ·

Dr. Sonya Friedman

with Guy Kettelhack

Ballantine Books
New York

Library of Congress Catalog Card Number: 91-91089

ISBN: 0-345-37597-1

Cover design by William Geller

Cover photo by Harry Langdon

Manufactured in the United States of America

First Ballantine Books Edition: January 1992
10 9 8 7 6 5 4 3 2 1

To all the women I know and those I've yet to meet, may you have the courage to give up your fantasies so that you can expend your energies working on a far better reality for yourselves and all your children

"If you always do what you've always done,
you'll always get what you always got."

Ann Kaiser Stearns
Coming Back

Contents

Acknowledgments

THIS book deals with issues concerning women that I feel are complex. Therefore, it was important to me to express them carefully. I am grateful for all the help I received in bringing this work to fruition.

To Connie Clausen, my agent, who bravely took me by the hand and encouraged me during the shaping of the idea; to Margaret Danbrot, who helped give the idea form; and to Fredrica Friedman, my editor at Little, Brown, who gave me a road map toward a finished product that would be user-friendly in form and have integrity in content — I thank you all.

To Guy Kettelhack, a writer who spoke and felt my language, and who made our time together a joy. His gift of professional skills and loving manner was a rare find indeed. This book could not have been completed without him.

To my friends, who always allow themselves to be called upon to read, to comment, to let me use their life stories, and to massage my spirit when it is sagging: Marilyn Barnett, Barbara Kopitz, Arlene Altman, Joan Peven Smith, Iris Kaufman LaJoi, Michael Stein, Dr. Herb Silverman, Dave Bell, Betsy Farley, and Susan Grode. I feel blessed having you as my voluntary extended family.

And to my family, who I am sure sometimes scratch their heads, asking, "What is she up to now?" Thanks for always saying, "You can do it."

On a Clear Day
You Can See Yourself

■■■■■■■■■■■■■■■

Introduction

THIS is a book about making choices.

Maybe that doesn't sound like a new idea. Certainly a book directed to *women* about making choices may seem to cover familiar territory. We've heard from feminists for nearly thirty years now that we have the right to choose exactly how to live our lives, to get out from under the feminine yoke that centuries of male-dominated culture have thrust upon us.

So why do we need a book on choice now?

We certainly aren't where — or who — we used to be. As a recent cover article in *Time* magazine, "Women Face the '90s," proclaimed, "a vast majority [of women today] revels in the breakthroughs made during the past quarter-century: the explosion of roles for women, their far greater participation in the country's political and intellectual life, the many options that have come to replace their confinement to homemaking." Not all of women's struggles in the past three decades have been in vain. Women have a voice and a presence in today's world that we never had before.

And yet the issue of making our own choices has never been greater than it is today. Perhaps a lot of women (and men, for that matter) have gone into retreat for the very reason that so many old assumptions about us have been dislodged — or at least given a jolt so that we're starting to question them. Told that we can be whoever we want to be, a lot of women feel stymied, even terrified, and stuck in their tracks. Exhorted to make a journey of self-discovery, many women are simply baffled. What exactly does that mean? How do you make that kind of journey? And will it make you happy? "Self-discovery" and "making choices" sound fine on the face of it. But nobody has really told us, in ways we can clearly understand and implement, how to become what we dream of becoming: satisfied, fulfilled, at peace with who we are.

It's clear to me as a clinical psychologist, television talk-show host, and frequent lecturer to thousands of women across the country that women still aren't happy, despite the undeniable gains we've made. There is an ache for fulfillment that seems, if anything, to have intensified in the twenty-seven years since Betty Friedan woke us up to the sexist ties that bound us in *The Feminine Mystique.* This ache is often hidden beneath fear — a fear that actually changing your life to make it what *you* want it to be is more than you can really handle. I know this fear because I've felt it — and overcome it. I know what the struggle toward self-realization feels like because I grapple with it every day of my life. As a close observer of our culture for the past three decades, I've seen, listened to, and tried to help thousands of women who are facing the same struggle toward self-realization. And I've written about it.

In *Men Are Just Desserts,* I asked women to see themselves as the "main course" in their own lives, to see that they, not the men they loved, must direct their own lives. In *Smart Cookies Don't Crumble*, I wanted women to see that while life presents any number of obstacles and setbacks, they can be negotiated, and women need to learn to negotiate them if they are to move ahead. In *A Hero Is More than Just a Sandwich*, I talked about the fact that love is an acquired taste, that other people define love for us and that, often, our early experiences, even those that were abusive, may be misinterpreted by us as love since they're all we ever knew. It was a plea to women to examine carefully the contents of love and not just the label; to define love for themselves instead of accepting someone else's definition, so that they would feel cherished and respected when they heard the words "I love you."

In many ways, *On a Clear Day You Can See Yourself* is the culmination of these preceding books. What we need now, more than ever, is clarity about ourselves and who we can be. We need, once and for all, to extricate ourselves from the myths so many women still cling to out of habit or fear or ignorance, myths that keep us "girls" and prevent us from becoming as fulfilled and satisfied as we deserve to be. Learning, truly, to *see* yourself is the crucial first step to building any kind of fulfilling life. While my message has always been that we need to discover our own inner direction before we can live satisfying lives, it's now time to apply that message more broadly to what it means to become a woman — what it means, really, to grow up.

The child in us sometimes gets disgruntled at the thought of growing up: isn't becoming adult a pretty grim business? Who wants the responsibility of being a grown-up? Who wants to go through life with furrowed brow, worrying about bills, taking care of other people, holding down a job, becoming self-supporting, saving money, showing up on time, making adult decisions? For any number of reasons — many of which we'll explore in this book — women are peculiarly resistant to the idea of taking responsibility for themselves in a way they imagine to be grown up. Centuries of conditioning tell us that, really, our goal is to be taken care of. Taking full responsibility for yourself may deeply strike you not only as grim, for many women it can seem vaguely unnatural.

It's no wonder growing up has proved so elusive to the thousands of women I've heard express their ache to me. They've been saddled by somebody else's idea of what growing up means. It's never occurred to them to create their own definition. Not that there aren't some universals that separate woman from girl; as you will see, there are a number of hard facts that we have to face if we're to make that passage to true adulthood. But the goal isn't to turn into some stern, gray, burdened grown-up. The goal is to become as full and unique a human being as you can, to discover and then live up to your own unique potential as a woman.

Growing up is something we all desperately need to do. Why? Because you can't be happy until you've grown up. You can't have a chance of lasting satisfaction in your life until you accept responsibility for your own life as completely as possible — which is my definition of growing up.

Betty Friedan helped to identify the bafflement and ache felt by so many women today in her 1981 book *The Second Stage*, which made it clear that women were ready for something deeper than, and different from, the feminism that ensued after *The Feminine Mystique*. Friedan asked in *The Second Stage* that feminists go beyond sexual politics, which saw men as the enemy, and embrace *all* the options open to us, including motherhood and homemaking. Some feminists saw this as backtracking;

others interpreted her message to mean that we should try to have it all (although most of us who *did* try have given up in exhaustion).

In fact, Friedan's message is only now becoming clear, ten years later, and it's different from either of the above interpretations. She is inviting us to be *who we want to be*, and if that includes, or is even limited to, motherhood *or* the boardroom, fine. The point is to allow us to follow whatever path we wish to follow, not to knuckle under to whatever the prevailing politically correct pressure happens to be. *The Second Stage* asks that women look to achieve balance in our lives, to celebrate our nurturing traits as well as our assertive ones. This new feminism doesn't require women to become men; it allows us to be women in a fuller, wider, and more permissive sense than we've known before.

What a lovely idea this balance is! But how, exactly, do we go about achieving it?

That's what *On a Clear Day You Can See Yourself* will tell you.

Too many of us grow old before we grow up. I've learned in my own life, and from the experience of thousands of women, that our happiness depends on how well we grow up. But what exactly *is* growing up? How do you do it?

The first step is to develop as much clarity about yourself as you can. This doesn't only mean taking stock of your particular circumstances right now (although that is important); it means looking at some of your hidden assumptions that may be keeping you on a lifetrack you don't really want to be following. What we'll examine in the first chapter is the most damaging assumption women commonly make about themselves, what I call the Feminine Mistake: thinking — believing — that direction and fulfillment come from outside yourself. This is how we've seen and stymied ourselves for decades, no matter what prevailing message we were told to espouse. But gaining an appreciation for the power and pervasiveness of that mistake is only the beginning. It sets us up for a number of other hard truths, which we'll examine in the second chapter of this book.

Those hard truths, a woman's Facts of Life, will explode many of the myths our Feminine Mistake has encouraged us to believe: Myths about how and where to find happiness, love, fulfillment. Myths that have led to all the misery women have known in their lives, all the misery that continues to plague us today. And we'll start, right away, to see how to begin to free ourselves from these myths, awakening to what are sometimes very subtle restraints that have needlessly held us back. The Facts of Life may surprise you, but they'll set the path for the rest of our journey — a journey that should prove to your own satisfaction that these are indeed facts.

The next leg of that journey will help you to apply the principles of self-reliance you'll be learning to the sometimes terrifying prospect of making actual changes in your life. How do you decide exactly what changes to make? What changes have the best chance of fulfilling you? Chapter 3, with its Four Rs of positive action, will start you on your way.

We'll then explore some specific ways to develop the inner strength you need to *sustain* positive changes once you start to make them. Growing up means a new kind of getting tough: developing the pragmatism and discipline to face life on its own terms is essential to making changes in your life that will last. In chapter 4 you'll learn some "emotional fitness" exercises to help you do exactly that.

Next, we'll focus on making decisions in ways you may never have thought of before. You'll have some ground rules by now about the importance of relying on your own instincts, desires, and needs, and some indication about how to start to fulfill them. In chapter 5 you'll take a look at the impact your decisions can have, not only on your own life, but on the lives of people around you. You will learn on this leg of our journey how your decisions connect you to the world and affirm the joy and responsibility of those connections. A satisfying life does not develop in isolation, as the following stops on our voyage will make even more clear.

This is not a book about dealing with men, and yet because most women's ideas of happiness are bound up in their expectations of love, and because women never sabotage their happiness more than when they get involved with men, we need to face the man/woman dilemma head-on, from the perspective of self-reliance. Can our new principles help us in love? In chapters 6 and 7 we'll carefully examine what life "with him" and "without him" can mean to a grown-up woman and offer ways of nurturing yourself, and keeping your integrity, as an independent woman, in or out of love.

We'll then take a turn into the wider world of work — another mine-laden territory for most women, another area where our self-esteem can be very shaky. Never have more women *had* to work, never has it been more important to develop a healthy sense of what work can mean in your life. Whether you're in it for power, the adventure it gives you, the creative outlet it can afford, or simply to pay the rent, bringing a grown-up perspective to your career or job means learning to see and use your work time in new ways. Making your life meaningful in the workplace, where most of us spend the greater part of our waking hours, presents some special challenges to women, which I'll show you how to face in chapter 8.

By the time we pull into the final depot of our trip — chapter 9, "Don't Make a Wish, Make a Life" — you'll be able to begin to assess what you've learned about self-reliance and start to monitor your own progress toward self-definition.

Is the journey worth it? I hope and expect the answer will be self-evident by the time you've reached the end of this book. You'll have the tools to make your own blueprint for healthy change, your own guide to taking the reins of your life, and you'll have learned to start directing yourself to the fulfillment each woman longs for and deserves. In short, you'll have begun to create a "clear day" for yourself — to find the clarity you need to see who you really are and what you can do to become who you want to be.

1

●●●●●●●●●●●●●●●●●

The Feminine Mistake

●●●●●●●●●●●●●●●●●●●●●●●

WOMEN have changed enormously in the past three decades . . . haven't we?

Certainly our "progress" from the close-knit-family fifties through the bra-burning sixties, the executive seventies, and the have-it-all eighties seems a fairly clear record of change. But what, really, did change?

Appearances, certainly. However, throughout all these decades, women have heard one unceasing message, whether it was from Gloria Steinem or Phyllis Schafly — or their lovers, husbands, bosses, fathers, or mothers: "Follow what *I* tell you to do and you'll be all right." From the kitchen to the bedroom to the boardroom, women have tried desperately to carry out someone else's instructions. Furthermore, women have allowed these instructions to be imprinted on their psyches as if they were some genetic code, an inescapable formula, a recipe that you had no choice but to follow if you wanted to be happy. What these codes, these instructions, urged us to do was to turn over our lives and our wills and our thinking to someone or something other than ourselves.

In the fifties, our parents set our course: we promised to "obey" them up until we got married, when we promised to "obey" our husbands. We went from our bed at home to our husband's bed without ever understanding — or, for most of us, daring to imagine — what it might be like to be a person in our own right. Girls didn't leave home until they got married and, in many cases, felt very strongly that to graduate from college without an "MRS." was to be a failure.

In the sixties, many of us broke these restrictive bonds and became what felt like "free." Sexual freedom, experimenting with drugs and alternative life-styles, and, perhaps above all, the heady anarchy of rebellion leveled a lot of old assumptions. But many of us were so anxious to say yes that we forgot how to say no and ended up feeling lonely and unhappy, using our bodies as a way of breaking down the barriers that we later learned could truly be removed only through time and care. We discovered there were no quick routes to enlightenment, intimacy, love, satisfaction.

The seventies had us aching for careers. "Jobs" would no longer do; every woman felt inadequate unless she was on the path toward becoming a CEO. Women who chose to stay home with their children were looked down on, and few women had the courage to say they enjoyed being housewives. The message was, "Be a man!" — even for women.

In the eighties, we weren't satisfied with competing with men; now we had to have "everything." Letty Cottin Pogrebin put things into perspective when she said that "Superwomen had become Super-exhausted." She was right. In clinicians' offices today, everyone talks about being tired, irritable, unable to do two full-time shifts, one at work and the other at home. The modern woman is now often as unhappy as women whose malaise Betty Friedan talked about in *The Feminine Mystique*.

Some women long for the good ol' days. In fact, we have a term for a reactionary phenomenon: retrofeminism. There is, suddenly, a hunger for home and hearth, comfort foods, and mommy and daddy with the kids watching sitcoms on the TV. The Huxtables have replaced the Ricardos, but we're drawn back to a time most of us can only dimly remember — the fifties, which women have spent thirty years trying to escape! "It's a jungle out there," many women say now. "I want to go home."

What has "'liberation'' wrought? What it *hasn't* wrought is any real change from the "follow the leader" game we started out playing however many years ago. Obviously not every woman was affected equally by the trends in the neatly characterized decades I've described above; depending on our ages and backgrounds, we have different experiences in acculturation. But few of us have escaped the underlying external message in whatever acculturation *did* affect us: "Do what I tell you to do if you want to be happy."

■■■■■■■■■■■■■■

The Courage to Trust in Yourself

In too many ways, we are exactly where we have always been: searching for answers outside ourselves, clinging to the known, fearful of stepping out and speaking for ourselves as individuals, trying again and again to fit ourselves into whatever the prevailing notion of fulfillment is supposed to be. In truth, not all women want to be married. Some don't even especially want men in their lives. Some women don't want careers; they don't even want to work if they don't have to. Some women know they cannot manage a full-time career and a marriage at the same time. They welcome the idea of a Mommy Track. Who is to say what is right for you if not *you?* Who is it more logical to trust than yourself to make the major decisions that will shape your life and your legacy?

It seems obvious that each of us individually deserves to be the arbiters of our own lives. But it is equally obvious to me that we need help in learning how to take back the reins. One of my clients woke up literally screaming one morning as she realized her fortieth birthday was only two weeks away. Why was she screaming? What was she afraid of? Not just of getting old, but of not having fulfilled her destiny — of not having hooked up with a man and a house and kids and the "normal" life she was supposed to have achieved by now. Of not having followed the voice she'd internalized as a child: "Be a good little girl, do what little girls are supposed to do, and you'll get the prize. Trust me," the voice says, "and you'll get the life every little girl should grow up to have." This woman, on the verge of forty, woke up screaming because she'd tried to do everything "little girls" were supposed to do, but she'd obviously failed. She was still alone — and miserable.

The voice she couldn't bring herself to follow was her own. And, for most of us, that's our problem, too: the voices we haven't followed are our *own* voices. The trust we have not developed is trust in ourselves. The feminine mistake we've made is thinking it could ever be otherwise — that we could ever find outside ourselves what can be discovered only within. We unconsciously made a pact with ourselves to follow directions others set for us — whatever directions were current at the time. This gave us a deeply ingrained sense that we were entitled to certain rights: since we had done what we were supposed to do, weren't we entitled to the perfect man, the perfect marriage, the perfect life-style? Sure, we knew it would take work, but we suspected that work would pretty much take care of itself, as long as we kept ourselves attractive, receptive, and caring. Even when we outwardly espouse more "advanced" goals, we often find that our inner little-girl selves are still hoping to be rewarded for being "good." Everything will fall into place, the little girl in us believes. It's just a matter of waiting and hoping.

Unfortunately, however, this passivity, whether inner or outer, has become the biggest obstacle to getting what we want; it is not the best means of achieving what we want that we secretly believe it is. Nothing has held us back more tragically than our own passivity — or our own blind faith, an unthinking prejudice, that if we only wait long enough, someone or something will save us and make things better.

This may seem an odd time for an old joke, but bear with me: it makes the point nicely.

A dam has broken near a town and the townspeople start to evacuate, everyone except one woman who refuses to budge. "I've put my faith in God," she says. "He'll save me." The water comes rushing in and her house is deluged. She has to climb onto her roof to survive. Someone in a rowboat comes by and offers to take her away. "No," she says, "God will save me." The waters rise so that the woman has to climb on top of her chimney to get above them. People in a rubber raft float by and they throw out a life preserver. But the woman won't budge. "God will save me," she says. Finally a helicopter descends and throws down a rope ladder. Although she's now treading water, the woman still won't accept help. "God will save . . . ," she gurgles, as she goes under and drowns.

Now she's up at the Pearly Gates and she's pretty upset. She confronts the Almighty: "I had faith in you, God. Why didn't you save me?"

"What do you think I was trying to do?" God retorts. "I sent you a rowboat, a life raft, and a helicopter!"

Whatever you may think of that joke (I know it's an

old warhorse), it points out a very valuable lesson about many women who, like our fearful thirty-nine-year-old, deeply believe that faith — (or their bosses, lovers, husbands, best friends, or some other "savior") will make things all right again. We may hide this belief from ourselves through the staunchest outward defiance, but it's the rare woman who wasn't brought up to think that ultimately happiness is brought to you by someone else. You may, for example, be extraordinarily sophisticated psychologically about why you always end up with the wrong job or the wrong man or make bad financial decisions, but somehow this impressive knowledge doesn't seem to prevent you from getting into still *more* job, man, and money problems. Knowledge can't, of itself, always help us to get to the root of what's causing the mess in our lives: what's causing that mess is usually the deeply imbedded belief that we don't really have the power to provide *ourselves* with what we need.

When happiness doesn't come from outside — or when it seems to come, but then quickly disappears — we experience a deeply felt loss of self. It's not only women who break up with, or get divorced from, men who experience this; women who adamantly remain single, or who devote themselves single-mindedly to their careers, or who may be married but see their marriage as a chore to be dealt with through total self-sacrifice — all these women are often responding to an inner voice that tells them they're inadequate unless they adhere to whatever particular set of rules they've been told to follow.

Such a response is blinding. There are any number of rowboats and life rafts and helicopters we miss when we cling to passive faith or to a strict notion of self-sacrifice — or a strict notion of just about anything. There are any number of wonderful opportunities we miss as we cling to the myths our internalized voices want us to embrace.

You have the greatest chance of being happy when the voice you respond to is your *own* voice. That's the secret women have been keeping from themselves. Each of us is someone special and unique and worthy of careful, individual nurturing. None of us has exactly the same road to happiness as anyone else, despite what "they" have been telling us for decades.

Let's say you wake up to this secret. Isn't that enough to get you to change your life right now, right away? Or do you still freeze at the thought of changing to rely on yourself?

■■■■■■■■■■■■■■

Fear of Change

If you're still wary of the changes that self-reliance seems to entail, you belong to a very large group. It's no wonder you're scared — or simply exhausted at the prospect of anything that sounds as if it would mean sweeping change. You've been told to scramble after so many disparate goals in the past two or three decades that it's no wonder if you've grown mistrustful of any new "instructions" hurled at you. Why, for that matter, should you trust my advice over anyone else's?

Actually, it's not my advice I want you, ultimately, to follow. It's the advice you give yourself that counts. All I hope to do is help you to develop the trust in yourself first to find, then to *heed* your own voice, your own self. If you find yourself depressed because outside answers don't seem to be working anymore, count yourself lucky: it means you're on the verge of an important awakening. However painful your route to this awakening has been, you're finally learning a simple and very instructive fact: "They" don't have the answer to your life. That answer has to lie somewhere else — in *you*.

We may be frightened to think that "somewhere else"

is in ourselves. But where else is there to look? Who could possibly know you better than you? We tried to forge our identities at other people's direction, and that hasn't worked. Perhaps we've got to look at our lives from a different vantage point. It's a new idea, and also, probably, a painful one. You may never have asked yourself some of the questions you now find you need to ask: What if he leaves? Who am I then? What if I'm fired? Who am I then? What happens when the kids grow up and I'm alone? What happens if I decide not to have kids at all?

Depending on yourself may still seem too foreign an idea. It could never be enough, we fear, simply to be ourselves — to trust in who *we* are, what *we* want, to make our *own* lives happen. We have been brought up to look outside for direction, whether in service to traditional values or radical feminism. It has become a reflex to take our cues from Out There.

But that's the biggest feminine mistake of all.

In fact, there are any number of "life rafts" and "rowboats" and "helicopters" out there to help you once you've made the decision to live your own life; any number of ways out of whatever rut you're in, chances to be helped, chances to get somewhere better. But we can't begin to recognize the help available to us until we've formed a vision of the new selves we want to be. And forming that vision takes a kind of inner work you may not yet have learned to do.

■■■■■■■■■■■■■

From Girl into Woman

Many women haven't learned to put in the spadework necessary to find themselves, to develop a vision and then mold their lives so that the vision becomes reality. Our biggest, and initially hardest, job is to take the clearest look we can at ourselves, and then to accept and build from what we see. From this comes self-knowledge — and the chance of fulfillment we're after.

This may be the first time you've really attempted to take that objective view: to see how you got where you are, what you really want for yourself, and then, crucially, how to change so that you've got a chance of getting what you want. Doing all this comprises the task and promise of this book. I am going to help you face the most difficult but — I promise — the most rewarding task you've ever faced. It's one you'll never stop facing once you've begun it. Certainly I haven't stopped facing it: I continue to struggle with this process every day of my life. What is it, the task and the process? *Turning from girl into woman.* The objective view that begins to make this possible will bring you closer to the promise of this book's title: you'll be on the way to achieving the clarity to truly *see* yourself, without fear, without harsh judgment, with love, and with the confidence that you can turn who you see into who you want to be. Achieving this "clear day" automatically will increase that all-important sense of self-confidence: that clarity will teach you that you *do* have the resources to direct your own life, to live the way you truly want to live. It's at this moment that you enter womanhood: a state, as you may already know, all too few "girls" really achieve.

It doesn't matter what age you are; we can be girls in our forties, fifties, sixties, or seventies. (We can be women at twenty-five.) It also doesn't matter whether you've grown up espousing traditional values or strongly feminist views. You can be a girl rather than a woman in either case. The misconceptions to which each extreme usually clings can be readily defined, even if, because of our own denial, they can be initially difficult to detect in ourselves. As I said before, it often doesn't matter how sophisticated or advanced the views you express to the world are, or how much you understand that it's up to you to make your own life better, how much you intellectually or rationally realize that you can't depend on someone else for happiness. The beliefs I'm talking about are so deeply ingrained that we sometimes block them from our own conscious awareness. But, alas, they're very often there — and directing us.

There are two poles of belief; you may veer to one or the other. As old-fashioned as they may sound, they are rampantly alive in far too many women. One pole is what I call a "Miss-conception," the idea I've already described that if we only do the right things, we're *entitled* to a good life. This idea was planted when women (and perhaps you) thought of themselves as "Miss," with all the old-fashioned propriety and passivity that term of address implies. The other pole is more rebellious but just as limiting: it's what I call a "Ms-understanding." It's the idea that we should never allow anyone to help us or in any way infiltrate our lives; we've got to keep our guard up or we'll get hurt. Ms-understandings are often planted in women who outwardly rejoiced at the institution of the feminist term of address "Ms" but whose angry feminism hides a deeper fear of intimacy.

What believers in the Miss-conception and the Ms-understanding have in common is that they are both girls; neither is a full, rounded woman. Fear holds each back from growth: in the "Miss," it is the fear of not being able to accomplish anything on her own; in the "Ms," it is a fear of becoming too dependent. A healthy *woman*, on the other hand, creates balance in her life between intimacy (the ability to give of herself in love, to care and empathize and nurture) and independence (the ability to trust her own instincts, protect her own best interests, and follow the path she has set for herself). The healthy woman is self-protective without being paranoid or overly defensive; she is caring without turning herself into a doormat. It is very clear to me that the healthy woman reserves a piece of herself *for* herself: she nurtures and cherishes the core of who she is, and makes that core inviolable, able to withstand the attack of any man, outside credo, or internalized voice.

■■■■■■■■■■■■■■

Taking Stock

Becoming this healthy woman is, however, an ongoing process, one that requires vigilance. Moving toward the ideal is what engenders health: you probably won't ever *be* that ideal, but striving to reach it will give your life purpose and satisfaction. But here is one guarantee: you can't grow the first millimeter toward becoming that balanced, healthy woman without taking realistic stock of who and where you are right now. The first step in the journey to finding fulfillment is to define what that fulfillment would consist of *for you*, but you can't begin to come up with that definition until you've taken stock of your life.

This is essential for a simple reason: you can't plan what to do with your life if you don't have a clear idea of what you're working with. And what you're working with is *you*: all the potential, experience, assets, and liabilities that are part of you. I want you to look at and start taking care of yourself with the same clarity and interest and devotion you probably lavish on your plants — and your family, lover or spouse, children, friends, coworkers, or boss. It may never have occurred to you to take the time to do this; if you're like the majority of women, it may seem self-indulgent to pay attention to yourself, to make *you* your priority. Everyone else needs you too much, don't they? And you may have felt that by meeting everybody else's needs, you produced your own security.

But real security doesn't come that way.

You need yourself more than anyone else needs you. And I want you to meet that need, *your* need.

The goal of taking stock of your life is not to tear yourself down or lead you to despair over your inadequacies. I do not invite you to berate yourself. I ask only, in this first step, that you take a look at what's there, at your assets as well as your liabilities. This means telling the story of your life to yourself in a new way. By learning not to cringe at the uncomfortable, painful parts — learning simply to *see*, without judging, what has formed you and what influences you now — you can begin to clear your own slate. You begin to see the clay you've got to work with. That clay is very precious. It is, in fact, the most precious asset you've got, and you can depend on it being an asset from the very start. It is your *life*.

To appreciate the vastness, the richness of this gift, it helps to appraise it, to set it in context. By standing outside yourself and looking in the "window," you can create enough distance really to see yourself: who you were, who you are, and who you wish to be. That's the goal of "meeting yourself": to see and appreciate the contours of your own life.

This stock-taking is crucial and ongoing. I'm not exempt from it; in fact, as many times as I've combed my past to understand the obstacles I continue to face, I find it's always worthwhile to take another look. There's always something I've missed, something new to learn. I took stock again recently, concentrating on my childhood, and uncovered some new lessons. Different as the circumstances of my life may be from yours, I think you'll identify very strongly with most of the feelings. Do for yourself what I'm about to do now: tell your story. Look in it for clues. Think of it in the light of what we've already explored so far in this chapter: be sensitive to the Feminine Mistake we're all tempted to make. How much were you responding to somebody else's voice? How much did you respond to your own?

These mileposts on my path from girl to woman show some of the ways I learned about these issues. Some of them may surprise you. I hope all will be resonant.

■■■■■■■■■■■■■■■

My Story

Whether you know me from TV, radio, or my books or are meeting me for the first time in this book, you probably wouldn't guess that I had the background I did. I have been blessed with an immense curiosity about the world, an immense desire to live my life as fully and consciously as possible, and this desire has taken me a long way. But sometimes, when I catch a glimpse of myself on TV, I laugh a little: "Who is that woman?" I wonder. "Can she really be me? Where did she learn all that self-confidence?" And I think back to when Sonya Friedman was a good deal less sure of herself.

The woman I am today, and the public image I project, have grown from a basic understanding, a message I phrase to myself as follows: Don't count on others to hand your life to you. To some degree we all learn this early. We may see, as children, that we've got to earn our allowance by doing chores or practice the piano before we can play it well. In my case, the lesson was a bit more basic. Even *love* wasn't handed to me. I know I'm not unique; you too may have felt as I did — unloved, unwanted, and wondering if my mother and father were really my parents. My earliest memory is of my mother and father having a fight: a chair was thrown, my father's nose began to bleed, he yelled and threatened. I remember running over to my mother to cover her ears so she wouldn't hear the terrible things my father was shouting. I was three years old when my parents separated.

My mother and I moved into my grandparents' three-bedroom apartment in Brooklyn, which was already occupied by two uncles and an aunt. The only child in this crowd of adults, I seemed to have three mothers and three fathers, few of whom agreed with each other about how I was to be raised. It was a confusing life for a three-year-old. In those days, the wartime early 1940s, the greatest shame for a "nice Jewish girl" like my mother was to be divorced. It was essential that we protect her reputation, which I was instructed to do by answering when asked about my father that he had been killed in the war. My father was a taboo subject in the house. Whenever I ventured a question about him, my mother abruptly said he wasn't interested in me and she didn't want to talk about him.

My mother eventually remarried, and we moved into her new husband's home. Ben was a widower with a fourteen-year-old daughter, Elaine, three years older than I. She had had a father all to herself; now she resented having to share him. My mother too was not willing to share. She carped and badgered and complained so much about Elaine that she left within a year to live with cousins in Arizona. I don't think Ben ever forgave my mother; I know he retaliated by never speaking to me unless it was absolutely necessary. There was ice between Ben and me, fire between Ben and my mother.

I don't remember a time in my childhood when I didn't feel as if I lived in an armed camp. Fights between Ben and my mother were physical, often vicious. Sometimes my uncles would intervene to defend their sister, but they'd just make the battles larger. If I bought something new for myself, I was told to keep it a secret from Ben. I'd have to smuggle any new blouse or skirt into the house, cut off labels and tags, and hide whatever few new clothes I bought in the closet. I was never allowed to ask him for anything.

My mother was full of rage. She fought constantly with Ben out of frustration and disappointment with her life. By her mid-thirties she seemed a bitter, loveless woman. At the age of thirty-six she gave birth to twin baby girls. Despite her own dependency and the beginning of her physical and mental deterioration, she found herself with two helpless infants — a situation that turned me into part-time mother. When I wasn't in school, I was taking care of the babies. My mother couldn't manage them on her own.

Things worsened between Ben and my mother. Once, late at night, he broke into my room and told me to get out of the house because my mother was violent, crazy. He opened a window and called to the neighbors for help. From time to time he'd leave and stay with a brother. When this happened, I'd be appointed to act as go-between, pleading with him to come back so that he wouldn't leave us without the wherewithal to take care of ourselves and the babies.

In pleading with him, I would go through a whole litany of apologies — apologies my family felt would warm him to return. I'd say everything was my fault, that if I hadn't been such a fresh kid things would have been easier at home. I would promise to be good and beg him to come back. Once he was kind enough to point out that it wasn't my fault that things were going wrong, that he'd treated me with such coldness because of what my mother had done to his daughter. I was so grateful for this kind scrap of truth! It allowed me to blame myself a little less, feel less crazy. By this time, I was beginning to believe my own apologies, to believe I *was* the cause of the heart-breaking mess our family had become.

It's no surprise that I grew up feeling needy, lonely, unwanted, unloved, and angry that the people closest to me couldn't give me what I desperately wanted: a home and a loving family like the ones I saw in the "Dick and Jane" readers at school. It was a terrible, searing pain — and yet it was a pain that I now realize taught me one of the most valuable lessons I've ever learned.

■ ■ ■ ■ ■ ■ ■ ■ ■ ■ ■ ■ ■ ■ ■

The Fork in the Road

My childhood had not taught me yet how to love — that lesson came much later. But it did teach me the truth I began this story with: You can't count on others to hand your life to you. Sometimes I saw this truth as bitter, but the fact that I did not allow it to capsize me, drain me of hope, drive me into myself, and squash any expectations I might ever have secretly nurtured for a happy, fulfilling life came from something I learned to do for myself. What was it?

I learned to keep a special part of myself safe. I learned to cherish something deep and secret in me. I learned to *believe* that I had something special to contribute to the world, and that evenutally I'd figure out how to bring it out into the light. Through some miracle, I knew deeply that despite how terrible I felt my life had been, it did not have to be terrible forever. *I had a choice.* This flicker of certainty, this inner knowledge that I had the power to save myself by believing in myself, is what has saved me. It saved me when I was a child, and it saves me now. It taught me that I am always approaching a fork in the road, and that there is always a more positive route I can take.

It was this flicker of self-belief that allowed me to over-come the feeling that I was a "bad seed." It allowed me to separate my needs from the needs of my terribly dys-functional family. I began to see that it was *they* who were so unhappy with themselves and their lives, so un-happy that they were unable to give me anything. It wasn't my fault that they were unable to give. I was even able to see that, in many ways, they were far needier than I. Because none of them had the *self-belief* I had discov-ered in myself, they were bereft, barren, dependent on *others* for satisfaction, and thus doomed to be dissatisfied. This was an insight, an understanding, that saved me. It taught me that, yes, I came from them, but I did not have to *be* them. I had a choice. I could choose a healthier path. I could make the right turn when I hit a fork in the road.

I can't tell you how freeing this sense is — if not of forgiving the hurt that was done to me, then at least of accepting what it was and that it doesn't have to hurt me now. Not that there haven't been some significant resid-ual negative effects. The strong expectations I learned to have of myself sometimes made me very rigid with my husband and children later on in life. My perfectionism can be damaging, and I'm continuing to learn how to soften its edges, become more flexible and tolerant of the people I'm closest to — as well as of myself. But the pro-cess of separating myself from my earliest roots, with forgiveness or at least understanding, has had some won-derful positive effects. I no longer fear that my past will run out in front of me and become my future. I do not have to turn into my embittered mother. I do not have to turn into my loveless father.

Which brings me to a much more recent fork in the road in my life. I had occasion last year to see the father who left me all those years ago. It taught me some new lessons — painful lessons about love. It shows me even more of what I need to acknowledge daily: I do not have to be held back by others' inadequacies. I can create love and happiness and fulfillment in my *own* life.

■■■■■■■■■■■■■■

Learning to Love

I visited my father in Blue Hill, Maine, on Father's Day a couple of years ago for the first time in many years. I'd harbored the secret hope that now, after all the pain and disappointment and growth I assumed we'd both undergone, I might be able to establish a new relationship with him. The truth was, I still hoped for a loving daddy; the secret was, I thought he'd embrace me with open arms and make up for the empty years after he'd abandoned me.

This was not to be. With barely a hello, he grumbled something about his will — how he hoped I wasn't planning to inherit anything from him, because he was leaving all his money to charity. Evidently he thought this was why I'd come. I realized there was nothing I could say that would change the way he viewed me. Something central in him had shut down long ago. I looked at the old man my father had become, sitting there, defiant, secure in his having laid his cards out on the table, secure in his having let me know in no uncertain terms that if his money was why I had come, I could leave. It was one of the most painful moments in my life, one in which the last vestige of the needy little girl inside me had to make a choice: to drown in that neediness, to drown in self-pity, or to take the other fork in the road. The path to acceptance. I realized with sudden clarity that my father had always feared intimacy. He had a basic distrust of life and had no love to give me or anyone else. He had never nurtured it, and the source of it had long ago dried up. I had to accept that the well I'd come to, the well of love I'd hoped to find after all these years, was completely arid.

Facing my father's lovelessness has meant facing something even harder: the difficulties I've had in my own life accepting and giving love. I had to look at aspects of my adult self I did not like: the coarse ambition, my desperate need to be recognized, the driven feeling I had always depended on to get me through any obstacle life presented. I realize it was only in my forties that I could soften to the point where I could be receptive: where the little girl in me could trust someone else enough to let go of her fear, open herself to love. Need was something with which I was intimately acquainted, and I'd spent my life attending to my needs. But love, the selflessness of it, the capacity to nurture and be nurtured implicit in it — these were traits it took me much longer to develop. I saw that unhealthy love is looking for completion, while healthy, mature love is synergistic: you start from a basis of liking yourself and feeling yourself to be whole, and *then* you offer to share that whole self with someone else who is also whole. The goal of love is to enrich who both of you are, not to fill up voids in either of you. Seeing my father again helped me to acknowledge that I did, after all, know what love was. It was vivid to me by its nearly complete absence in him. I didn't hate him, and I don't hate him now. I am sad for both my parents for what they've missed: having a life that includes love.

We may wish we had been treated differently than we were, but the bedrock truth is that we can't change how we were treated even one iota. The fork in the road all of us face is what to *do* with this hard truth. Do we become bitter, resentful, needy? Do we demand retribution — assert what we feel is our entitlement to a happy life because we were denied so much in our past? Or do we do something different? Do we take the path of acceptance, of an enlightened view of the damage we were caused — a view that teaches us that much of that damage can be repaired, transcended, lived with?

We've already seen in this chapter that we have a choice: as many "facts" as we've been taught to believe about ourselves, not only by our families, but by the larger society, we have the power to question those "facts" today, to see if they've led to assumptions that just aren't true and are needlessly holding us back.

You *can* go forward. You always have the power to choose that more positive fork in the road. And when you follow that path, you can find out some amazing things. Certainly I've learned some amazing things about my family — things that would have astonished the girl I once was. I have learned to be grateful to my father and mother. They gave me two wonderful gifts: the first is a good mind; the second, and far more precious, is the gift of life. They really gave me all I ever needed. I'm able to say, with complete sincerity, "Thanks, Mom and Dad. I'll take it from here."

■■■■■■■■■■■■■■

Telling Your Story to Yourself

I've brought you through the example of my own child-hood and the discovery of another piece of the puzzle I've made recently. Each year more pieces of that puzzle are revealed. Your own story undoubtedly has equally diffi-cult, painful memories: none of us has escaped pain in growing up — or, rather, growing *older*. Growing *up* — becoming a woman, not merely a superannuated girl — takes a special kind of effort, which is bolstered by de-veloping and nurturing the attitude I've been gradually spelling out in these pages: *your life is full of choice*. It is *always* full of choice. Even at your bleakest moments, you can resort to an inner sense of yourself, an inner hope and feeling of possibility; you can fan the flame of self that I promise is in each of us.

But first you have to find that flame. And you can find it by telling — or, as you'll see in a moment, retelling — your story. You may think you know your childhood; you may think you hold no secrets about your life from yourself. But looking at your life to learn from it requires some self-questioning you may never have attempted before. You can't begin to explore your life in this new, more productive way, however, if you aren't willing to risk finding some surprises — not all of them pleasant. You need to be willing to look beneath your resentments, beneath "what she did, what he did, what they did to me," to what *you* did. The point of looking at your past is to learn from it, not to berate yourself or anyone else for real or imagined inadequacies. Blame gets you nowhere; attempting to understand what fuels your resentments and fears is the key to moving ahead.

Take some time to recount the important events in your life. Organize your biography by answering the following questions, not just in your head, but on paper. Give yourself time to free-associate — and *think* — before you answer:

1. Who has helped me most in my life? What did I learn from this person that still helps me today?

2. Whom do I resent most from my past? What fears underlie these resentments?

3. What am I least proud of in my past behavior? What am I most proud of?

4. How does my past affect my present — and my expectations of the future? Do I feel held back by what I "never got"?"

5. What do I most want to change in my life today? Do I
believe I have the power to make this change?

It's all right to leave this biography open-ended. You
don't have to come up with explanations of every fear
or solutions to every problem that comes up in this retelling. It's the task of this book to help you do that.
But telling your story to yourself — by putting the emphasis on what you *learned* from your past, not merely
how your past hurt you — is the best first step you can
take toward creating that all-important vision of the
new you.

Our eyes open slowly to who we are — and who we
can be. Give yourself time. You've got all the resources
you need to make your life happier, fuller, and more
meaningful, but you don't have to uncover all of those
resources at once. I don't expect you to shed a lifetime of
restrictive conditioning overnight. Be patient with yourself. To the skeletal biography you've just begun by answering the five questions above, give yourself freer reign
now: write down your *feelings* about how your past has
affected you.

Take a moment to think about a particularly difficult
time you had in childhood or adulthood, an event or a
situation you know was crucial to who you are now.
Maybe it was something that caused you shame, something that hurt you. Maybe you felt betrayed, or felt you
betrayed someone else. Give yourself permission to meditate on that moment. Don't judge yourself; just let the
memories happen to you, let them pass through. What
was really going on? What happened beneath the hurt?
And what message did you learn from it? "Never trust,"
"Don't risk," "Hide your true feelings" are some common
negative messages that we learn from the difficult times
in our lives. What are the slogans you learned, and live

by now? Write them down so they're clear to you. "You're not enough," "You'll never make it on your own," "You're selfish" — there are any number of inner maxims and messages you may not realize you broadcast to yourself.

Don't let these voices depress you. Don't even argue with them for now. Just see what they are. All you're doing is seeking a clearer idea of what you're up against, to begin to identify some assumptions that have been holding you back. Your own story is full of the seeds of those assumptions, and as you travel with me on the rest of the journey I'm offering in this book, more will come up. However, what will also come up are ways to change those assumptions so that you can choose the right fork in the road for you, a fork that brings you a little closer to fulfillment.

That fulfillment becomes possible when you separate who you are from who you've been told you'd better be, or should be, or can't be. When you begin to take the kind of stock of yourself you're taking now, you begin to see that you've got power of your own, power unattached to anybody else. You do not have to look outside yourself for energy. You don't have to plug yourself into somebody else's current for direction. You can generate yourself. And that, in a nutshell, is the goal: to become a self-generating woman — self-reliant and confident in your own ability to meet life head-on.

Meeting life head-on starts when you begin to appreciate what you're bringing to your life. The legacy of your past is something you can't help bringing with you, which is why it's so important to try to learn from it. It's a rich source of clues about how you've learned to operate in the world today. The bad news is that much of how we learned to operate in the world is based on false, damaging assumptions — myths we may cling to because we were taught they were truth, but that have actually set up the biggest blocks to growth, and growing up, we face.

It's time to take a look at some of these myths and give you some reliable truths to replace them. Get ready for the "facts of life," coming up next.

2

....

The Facts of Life

....

SOME women grow old —
others grow up.

That's our first hard truth. As you saw in the last chapter, the Feminine Mistake is thinking that your role in
life is handed to you — that happiness comes from playing out a role from somebody else's script. And as you
probably saw in the retelling of your own life, you've
bought into that Feminine Mistake again and again. If
you expected happiness to come from outside and it
hasn't, you may feel stumped. Some women worry, cry,
complain, and blame; others suffer in silence. But no
woman who continues behaving in the same old ways
grows up. She simply grows older.

Hard as this truth is, however, it's not a helpful truth
if you respond to it guiltily, by tearing yourself down. "I
know I should be doing something about my life," you
might be saying, "but I just don't have the . . ." pick one:
Courage. Energy. Will. Talent. Intelligence. Money. Too
often you get bogged down because you've admitted

defeat before you started. Too often you react to a hot stove *only* by retracting your hand when it burns. I'd like you to do something more with that stove. I'd like you to take a look at it. See if you might be able to turn the heat down. See if it needs repairs. See if you need a new one.

We can grow only from who and where we are *right now*. Denying your past and your experience, or refusing to look at the realities of your life by attempting to wrest yourself violently away from it, can't change who you are inside. Ignoring or blindly changing your externals won't bring about lasting growth. Who you are inside will simply recreate the same destructive externals all over again — unless you pay attention to who you are inside, to what makes you *you*.

As I've already suggested, you have all the resources you need right now to begin a new, happier life. You won't become convinced of this, however, merely by hearing me tell you. You'll become convinced first by discovering your own resources for yourself, then by discovering you can use them — that you have, in fact, been using them to some degree all along, even if you weren't aware of it!

The journey you've embarked on in this book will take you to some surprising places. And the experience of reaching those places yourself will be far more magical, far more persuasive than any travel brochure or map I might set out for you. But just as it's usually foolish to set off on a major trip with no clue about where you're going, it's foolish to decide you're going to have a new life without investigating some sort of route beforehand. What I can offer you here are mileposts — and some warnings about common reefs and shoals to navigate around. These "facts of life" — there are nine of them — aren't only cautions, however. They're also goals. Not only do they distill what I've discovered to be true about the process of helping yourself to the best life you can have, they are perspectives to work *toward*. Just because you can list them in the space of half a page doesn't mean you can live them without expending any effort. Some of the following "facts" may appear to be self-evident, but the inner process of living in accordance with them takes work that isn't always easy. The work is worth it, however. You get a tremendous reward at the end.

You get to open the present of your life.

■■■■■■■■■■■■■■

The Present of Your Life

Present is a rich word in the two senses in which I invite you to think of it. It means "gift" and it means "now." That describes your life, too: it is a gift, and it is happening now.

As you read these words, you are living your life. Your life isn't something that's going to happen once you've rehearsed the right lines or saved up enough money or found the right man or landed the perfect job or given birth to a child. Your life is happening every moment; you can't escape or postpone it. What you're doing now is spending a portion of your life reading this book. I value the fact that you're *living* now as you read this, that every moment you spend with me as I take you on this journey is a precious moment — not because *I'm* with you, but because you're choosing to spend a portion of your life with me. I see this as a responsibility to tell you everything I know about fulfillment in the best way I know how. I don't want either of us to waste a moment — waste any part of the gift of our lives. I want us both to use that gift as well and as wisely as we know how.

That's the sense of responsibility, of urgency, of truthfulness and compassion and wisdom I want you to bring to yourself, not only as you read this book, but as you live your life beyond this book. None of the following Facts of Life is meant to intimidate you, criticize you, tear you down. I'm merely holding up a light to some truths that have been profoundly helpful to me and to many, many women I've known as friends, clients, and mentors. In the rest of this chapter I'll give you some examples of how these facts can affect your life — and in the rest of the book you'll begin to see them as the premises from which all chance of fulfillment grows — but for now, here they are in their bare form:

Fact 1. No one can bring your life to you.

Fact 2. No matter what you do in life, someone important to you isn't going to like it.

Fact 3. Though it's painful, rejection won't kill you — and it may even lead to growth.

Fact 4. Every choice means giving up something else.

Fact 5. Some people are not capable of giving you what you're trying to get from them.

Fact 6. The way you treat yourself sets the standard for others.

Fact 7. There are no quick fixes that can permanently change your life.

Fact 8. Life is on a rheostat, not an on/off switch.

Fact 9. Some problems cannot be solved, but you can make peace with them.

Don't be surprised if, in reading this list, you find yourself resisting some of the facts. You might even feel that the opposites to these assertions are the real truth — or at least the truth according to which you've been living your life until now. When we turn this list on its ear, however, we come up with some popular *myths*, which might run as follows:

Myth 1. There is always someone to rescue you.

Myth 2. You can always find a way to please everyone, including yourself.

Myth 3. Being rejected is the worst possible thing that can happen to you.

Myth 4. You can have it all, all the time.

Myth 5. If you try hard enough, you can always get from people what you want them to give you.

Myth 6. Even if you don't treat yourself very well, others will.

Myth 7. There are quick solutions to everything if you try hard enough to find them.

Myth 8. Life is either wonderful or terrible.

Myth 9. All problems can always be solved.

A number of these myths may not sound like myths at all. They may be "truths" you've held on to for most of your life — truths you're determined to continue to believe.

However, they are myths, I promise you. And the truths they hide are essential to face. Not simply because they *are* true, but because facing them will allow you to take your first steps to making your life better. Not all of the following facts lend themselves to exercises that you can practice to reinforce their message, but some do. Where applicable, I'll suggest some ways to practice these truths so that they can become part of a new, more positive — and vastly more productive — attitude.

Here they are, one by one, in a careful breakdown that

should reveal a lot to you about how, why, and where you've been holding yourself back. Settle back and let me take you on a 1990s "Pilgrim's Progress" for women:

Fact 1: *No one can bring your life to you.*

All of us can mope and pine and complain about our lack of advantages or lack of love. Each of us has a choice to see life as full of possibility — possibility that does not depend on waiting for someone else to bring us to "bloom."

Many women, even many who see themselves as liberated or independent, grow up with the unconscious expectation that they'll be taken care of, that their wishes will ultimately be granted and their needs anticipated. Some women are more conscious of this expectation: they announce that they're *entitled* to certain kinds of happiness — usually involving the right man, a happy and sexually fulfilled marriage, healthy children, a good home, enough money to be comfortable, and, more or less incidentally, a rewarding career or hobby. Granted, this may be an oversimplification: your expectations may not be quite so conventional. But it doesn't matter what the expectations *are*, it's that you have them to begin with.

Expecting something to happen means waiting for it to happen. It implies passivity. It is, moreover, a condition most women in this culture have been encouraged, from all sides, to espouse. It stems from the old idea that women are to be taken care of, with men, supposedly, doing the caretaking. Even if your own painful personal experience has put the lie to this, even if you've had one terrible love affair after another, one marriage after another, the prejudice that there's *still* a "Mr. Right" out there who'll take over the reins of your life may persist beyond all reason or evidence to the contrary. You may feel, still, that you've got a birthright to happiness that just hasn't been fulfilled yet. Battered but not quite completely disillusioned, you decide to hang on — and wait some more.

Wake up to a painful truth. No one is out there searching for you. No one has been named by fate to take over your life and make everything perfect. No one.

You could turn this into an occasion for serious depression — or you could do something else. Open your eyes and see the fork in the road I told you about in the last chapter. Make this an occasion to start directing your *own* life.

The inescapable truth is that each of us is at the center of his or her own universe. Every life is a play in which the lead character is center stage — and the lead character in your life is *you*. Perhaps you once convinced yourself you were a supporting player in your own life. Perhaps you put the spotlight on your husband or on your children. What happened when they withdrew their love and support, even temporarily? What happened when you saw them bridle at being trapped on *your* stage? What happened when you saw them want to play out their lives elsewhere? You felt abandoned. You had no star in your play, so the play threatened to fold. You cast about frantically for a replacement. The news is you've always had that replacement. It's you.

But isn't this a terribly cynical way of looking at your life, or anybody else's? I mean, if we are all in our own orbit, at the center of our own stages, how is love possible? How is it possible to share anything with anyone else? Does being in the center of your own life mean being selfish and self-centered?

Certainly this is what many women think who've been brought up to believe that selflessness is the greatest virtue to which they can aspire, that nurturing is the all-consuming trait of a happy, fulfilled woman. Nurturing is, no doubt about it, a marvelous trait, and women have a wonderful talent and capacity for it. But it cannot be our only trait — at least if it's always aimed outside ourselves. We have to nurture ourselves if we're to thrive, if we're to have any chance at happiness at all.

Love *is* possible between two people — it is possible among many people — even if you're each conscious that you're at the center of your own stage. It is not cynical to suggest that we are all important to ourselves, it is stating something essential about what it means to be a healthy adult! It is productive to be concerned with your own wishes, needs, duties, and responsibilities, and it's unreasonable to suppose that someone else should put you first, over the course of a lifetime, and live his life for you. It is unreasonable to suppose that your task is to do that for him. No one is entitled to unconditional love and approval from anyone else, and you can't expect that this love and approval will be available from other people whenever you need or want it. You cannot expect someone else to value your comfort, well-being, and happiness over his own. And while you may have certain legal claims over people in your life, you do not have absolute emotional rights to them, any more than you have an inalienable right to a Mercedes-Benz, an Yves St.-Laurent wardrobe, a six-figure salary, or a chalet in the Alps. You may *want* these things (and even be able to acquire them), but you are not entitled to them.

The belief that we are entitled to certain things is an immobilizing trap. It can shift the burden of responsibility of taking care of ourselves from us to others — and those others more often than not don't want it. Nor should they be blamed for not wanting it. It's hard enough to live your own life without taking on somebody else's!

This may seem very logical, but have you taken it to heart in your own life? When you look closely at your own expectations, how many of them have been bound up in the idea that some magical Someone or Something would descend suddenly from the sky and "make it all better"? The person who feels herself entitled in this way expects others to make up for the inadequacies in her life by coming in to change them, to take over her environment. If other people don't come through for her, she feels disappointed. She may view their absence as just one more proof that she's unlovable, that she's undeserving — unworthy of the love and attention she craves. She may experience the same kind of rage an infant feels when her pacifier is taken away or when she isn't fed or changed on time. She may feel hurt, but the thought never occurs to her that she might ease that hurt by changing her *own* behavior: her interest is in changing or luring or appealing to other people, so that they'll come through in the way she was taught they were going to.

The entitled person is trapped in a maddening, exhausting circle. Nothing is ever enough: no matter how much love, admiration, attention, success, or money the entitled woman receives, she can't appreciate it because she can't trust it will keep coming. Since she's convinced it has to come from an outside source, it's no wonder she doesn't trust that it will continue. What control does she have?

None. And that's just the point. When we start to view our lives as beginning with *us* — when we start to see ways of making *ourselves* happy — a magical change begins to occur, something far beyond the inevitable discovery that we are capable of providing for ourselves. We begin to feel a sense of sufficiency. We begin to see that we're not the helpless, hapless victims of whoever we can lure in to save us, take over our lives, give us what we need. We start to be, perhaps ironically, *less* self-absorbed in a negative way when we pay *more* attention to meeting our own needs. We free ourselves to be truly independent. And far from making us less capable of love, we become more capable of it — because we have more of it to give. Handing your own life to yourself is one of the most freeing things you can do. It requires turning one of the most basic messages women have ever received on its head — the message that salvation can come only from the outside. The truth is exactly the opposite. Lasting fulfillment is always the result of an "inside job"; the only trustworthy guide you have to fulfillment is *you*.

Fact 2: *No matter what you do in life, someone important to you isn't going to like it.*

Any choices we make affect the comfort zones of those around us. Sometimes we decide their comfort is more important than our own, other times we may feel our comfort needs to be attended to. But when we face major decisions in our life — and the need to make major changes — we have to have the courage to go ahead with them, even when, inevitably, they'll cause some discomfort in others.

I know a woman who was considering cosmetic surgery at forty-five. She had a job meeting the public that demanded that her looks stay "intact," but she was overworked and tired and feared losing her job. She wanted a face-lift. She was nervous; she knew it was expensive, but felt it would increase her self-confidence and feeling of well-being. She inched toward the idea that a little vanity wasn't a bad thing after all, especially when it would help her in her job. Then she told her husband what she was thinking about.

"Over my dead body!" he said. He was horrified. Why would she want to do something only fading stars and aging matrons and over-the-hill women in Las Vegas did?

Didn't she realize he loved her for herself? Why was she suddenly so insecure? The woman felt duly chastened. She repressed her desire to enhance her attractiveness. She told herself her husband was probably right — she was just being silly and self-centered. And, after all, her competence on her job was really more important than how she *looked*. . . .

A year later her husband announced at breakfast one morning that he was looking into having a hair-transplant and possibly getting the bags under his eyes removed. The woman looked at him incredulously. "But what about surgery being only for fading stars? What about that self-centered vanity you kept telling me about?" Her husband looked up from his paper and said, "I've changed my mind." His wife was resentful. "Thanks a *lot*," she thought. She was ready to launch into him when suddenly she stopped — and had a little awakening. She smiled to herself as she realized what she had done. She had reverted to a childlike stance, before. She had asked for *permission*, and like a parent who feels threatened by a child's request, her husband responded by acting like a negative father and said no. "What a great lesson I've learned!" she thought. "Ask for opinions, but not permission, when you are an adult." She then went ahead, on her own, with her plans for plastic surgery.

Only by coming to terms with the fact that people *do* tend to act in their own best interests could this woman begin to understand her husband's seeming contradictions: not only was she playing the child, but she missed the fact that her husband was looking after himself — both when he said no to her request (he later admitted that he felt threatened by her desire to look younger) and when he announced his own plans to seek surgery. When it had to do with *her* vanity, he felt threatened; when it had to do with *his*, he saw no objection. It's not that he was unusually selfish or inconsiderate; he's simply a human being, and, like most human beings, he followed his own instinct to look after himself. Once his wife realized this about him, she began to take steps to make sure her *own* interests were being attended to.

It's so hard for women to hold out for what they really want. We've been so battered into thinking that someone else knows what's best for us. When we finally do summon up the courage to bring up our decision to act, we're usually so tentative that we almost invite dissension. But when we're more sure of ourselves, when it seems clear that what we want to do is best for us, we can make a statement about what we plan to do, not ask a question about whether others think it's okay. Helping your mate deal with the consequences of a decision you've already made is often a lot healthier than pleading with him to "let" you do it.

No doubt you have already experienced the resistance of others — including those who claim to want the best for you — when you told them that you wanted to do something new or different. Why do they resist? Often because your change may require some adaptation on their part — they might have to accommodate to new circumstances. The thought of change breeds fear in most people. It threatens the status quo. And even if the status quo is uncomfortable, people often prefer it.

I'm not suggesting that you never take into account other people's wishes; of course you don't want to hurt people you love by doing something you think will make you happy and them miserable. But when you give yourself the time to see what their resistance is all about, you may discover it's nothing other than their own fear of change — and that should never be enough to keep you from pursuing those things in life that allow you growth, a sense of really being alive, a sense of real satisfaction.

We may not be entitled to happiness as something to be given to us *gratis*, but we're absolutely entitled to anything we acquire under our own steam, as a result of our own efforts. And, sometimes, if that makes other people uncomfortable, they too may have to grow a bit. By giving in to others' demands, you are staying in a rut — limiting not only your own growth, but often that of the people to whom you're acquiescing!

SUGGESTED EXERCISE

Make a list of some achievable desires you've kept yourself from fulfilling because they seemed self-indulgent: getting an expensive haircut; attending a play or a concert; buying yourself something you've always wanted but thought frivolous, such as a piece of clothing, jewelry, a glossy coffee-table art book — anything that has appealed to you but that makes you feel guilty to think of actually acquiring. Now, next to each item, write down *why* you feel guilty about the prospect of getting it for yourself. Then take a look at those reasons.

Are you afraid of what your husband or family or friends would say? Or, more generally, what "people" would think? How big a block *is* the prospect of other people's disapproval to your getting what you want?

Next, focus on one item on your list, one that you feel you can afford even if it means some scrimping, but one that you really desire, and tell yourself, "I deserve to please myself by getting this." Repeat it until it becomes automatic. Make a date with yourself to go out and get it — and keep the date. You'll be proving to yourself that you're capable of doing something you really want to do, with no thought for anyone but yourself. Whenever you look at this gift to yourself (or use it, wear it, or think of it), repeat to yourself the affirmation it represents: *"I am deserving."*

Fact 3: *Though it's painful, rejection won't kill*
you — and it may even lead to growth.

We all logically know the truth of this "fact," and yet we
act, so much of the time, as if that's exactly what rejection
will do: kill us. One of our greatest fears as women is the
fear of rejection. We've all felt the terrible pain of being
turned down, and for some of us the hurt was so bad that
we refused to place ourselves in positions where we could
be hurt again. We just gave up trying.

We're so attuned to the pain of rejection that it can
make us react in completely irrational ways. Have you
ever been pursued by a man you found frankly dull — not
especially attractive or interesting, with whom chemistry
was just lacking — and then stopped seeing him because
the relationship had nowhere to go? When your rejected
suitor started to pursue someone else, how did you feel?
If you're like a lot of women, you may have felt jealous!
Suddenly you discover all sorts of attractive traits in him
you never noticed before. Now, you're interpreting his
turning to another woman as rejection of you — even after
you rejected *him*.

Or perhaps you casually walked in and applied for a
job that really wasn't what you wanted, but you told yourself you needed the interview practice so you went
through with it anyway. The job didn't pay much and was
boring and far below your skill and experience level. But
when you didn't get it, how did you feel? Did the job no
longer seem dull or inappropriate? Didn't you feel a pang,
wondering how you could have been so cavalier about the
interview when perhaps the job might have been perfect
for you?

Why do we suddenly endow people who reject us
with wonderful qualities — even if we rejected them first?
Because acknowledging that someone doesn't want us

pushes a button: we feel we lose status in their eyes, and suddenly they become "better" than us — at least better than we thought they were. Otherwise, wouldn't they be pleading with us on bended knee to stay, or come back? (Even if you were the one who broke up a friendship, don't you maintain a secret desire that the rejected friend will always remain "available"?)

Creating a better life inevitably puts you into situations where you're vulnerable to rejection. It's important to get used to the idea that being turned down is a *disappointment*, not a mortal wound from which there is no hope of recovery. However, if you take a close look at your life, you have all the evidence you need that you can survive rejection. Who hasn't had to suffer it? When the boy of your dreams didn't ask you out in high school, when you didn't get the highest mark in the class on your paper, when you didn't get the first job you interviewed for — did you survive? (I assume you did, or you wouldn't be here now, reading this book!)

It may be hard to appreciate it as such, but rejection is more than survivable — it can be a great gift, because it's such a great teacher. It allows us to see that we can pull through struggle even when we "lose." It lets us see that we can grapple with disappointment and then move on.

You may not have gotten what you wanted, and that's too bad. Disappointment hurts. Perhaps you're a little battered and bruised, but those bruises will heal. And maybe you're a bit stronger for having gone through the experience of rejection and come out the other side. Rejection is a great teacher because it reminds us how many opportunities we have — that the one brass ring we thought had to be the answer didn't, after all, have to be the answer. Rejection teaches us that we live in a world of abundance. That if we don't get what we want this time, we can get something else. There is no end to the alternatives. There are as many opportunities to succeed and love and achieve as you are willing to explore.

Again, it means choosing the "positive" fork in the road — something you've always got the power to do.

Fact 4: Every choice means giving up something else.

If that sounds like deprivation, think of it in the terms I've just used: choosing one fork in the road means not taking the other one. This seems to be so logical that it hardly bears mentioning, but our lives are so rarely ruled by logic. If you're like many women, you do everything you can to hold on to all your options for as long as you can. The fear of making a choice can paralyze you to such a degree that you may have difficulty making the simplest ones: choosing what color to wear, what to have for dinner, which carpeting would be best for the room — to say nothing of what man to marry, what job to take, what life you want for yourself. Because most women have been conditioned to be accommodating, the thought of making a choice — which necessarily excludes other choices — can be terrifying. (It's not that some men don't suffer from the fear of choosing, too; it's just that the problem, in my experience, is epidemic in women.) Something in us tries desperately to have our cake and eat it too, or eat the cake and not gain weight. The illogic of this does little to dissuade us from thinking it might be possible just this once.

It isn't. To enjoy a piece of cake, you not only have to resign yourself to eating it — and facing its absence after you're eaten it — but you've got to add the calories to your daily allowance, decide how large a piece to have of which cake. Doing that means forsaking other cakes or foods, doesn't it? (It does if you decide you don't want to put on weight!) The point is, choosing one thing means *not* choosing another.

This dilemma is never more vivid than in the lives of women who put off (and put off and put off) having a baby — until the loudest sound they hear is the ticking of that famous "biological clock." When Betty, a client of mine, finally became pregnant — the pregnancy she'd planned for after years of agonizing over logistics and the right time and place — you might have thought, having made the Big Decision, she'd be at peace with herself. Instead she had night sweats. She was deluged with questions like a swarm of gnats: Should she stay home — leave her brokerage job for a year or more — with the baby? Should she hire a nanny and then continue to work? If she stayed home, would she find herself on the Mommy Track and lose all the career strides she'd worked so hard to make? If she went back to work, would she lose contact with her baby? Would her child end up hating her?

The hard nut of a truth Betty's questions kept trying to crack is simple: you can't be in two places at one time, you can't do two things at once. There are always two sides to the equation of making a choice: one is what you get, and one is what you give up to get it. Why do we fight so relentlessly against this simple truth? Because we're terrified. Terrified that we've made the wrong choice. That every move is irreversible. That we've sunk ourselves in quicksand: we've made the wrong choice and there's no going back. And if the choice does turn out to be wrong, who's going to take the blame? You! God forbid — that seems a fate worse than death! And it will continue to seem that way until you can say two magic words:

So what?

Sometimes decisions *are* irreversible, but usually they're not. And whether they are or aren't, our ability to adapt to change is much greater than we normally give ourselves credit for. The trick is to develop the perspective that it's okay to be wrong. It's okay to have made a mistake. It's okay to "fail." Every decision you make isn't only a statement of intent or direction, it's, at least potentially, an opportunity to learn a lesson. It's an opportunity to see what life can be like when you *choose* to change it, when you choose to direct its flow. The good news is that the more decisions you make, the better you get at making them. Slowly you discover ways of getting what you want without giving up something essential, without really depriving yourself.

Angela, a newly divorced forty-year-old mother with two preschool-age kids who despaired of being able to make ends meet on the alimony her husband paid her, made what she felt was the reasonable decision to get a part-time job. But she was scared: she hadn't worked since before she was married, and she was afraid she couldn't *do* anything now. She took the first job she was offered — waitressing at a coffee shop — feeling grateful that anyone had offered her anything. Unfortunately, her life turned into more of a disaster: the coffee shop was always frantically busy and Angela was exhausted every night when she got home — and a good part of her pay went into the baby-sitter's pocket. She felt trapped. But because she had proved to herself she *could* go out and get a job, the idea began to blossom that she might be able to find something better — maybe even work she could do at home. She finally got a phone sales job she could do from her living room. She learned she didn't have to stick out the restaurant job, that there were other, more manageable alternatives, opportunities she was capable of finding and meeting. She had taught herself that she had more than one option to choose from, and that she was *worthy* of a job on her own terms. The decision she made to change jobs to something she could do at home had a domino effect: now Angela has more faith in her decision-making powers, and it's positively affected all aspects of her life.

I see decision making in terms of a cost/benefit ratio: What are you giving up and what are you getting? What is the emotional cost to you (for example) of giving up a man you like but who you don't feel is "marriage material" or doesn't treat you well? Is it just the fear that you'll never meet another man? If so, you're shortchanging yourself. After all, if you attracted one man, you can attract others. You don't have to hold on to someone or something you don't feel is right for you: the cost isn't worth the benefit. What is the cost of staying in a dead-end job where you've got no chance for promotion or learning anything new? You have to ask yourself whether the limitations of the job are worth taking the risk of finding something better. What is the real benefit of "shopping 'til you drop" as a means of staving off depression? When the bills come, does it still seem worth it? Is an affair worth the potential cost of your marriage? Is the cost of a face-lift or breast augmentation worth the effects on your self-esteem? Only *you* have the answer. It's true that, in advance, we can only guess at the actual cost/benefit ratio. The outcome can't truly be known until after the fact. But we can make some pretty educated guesses. Some benefits, as is clear from the start, will be short-lived (the delight in that double scoop of Häagen Dazs ice cream, for example). At best they offer a quick emotional soothing, often followed by anger at yourself for eating impulsively — or "acting out" in any number of other ways (buying too much, being promiscuous, etc.). Some costs are lifelong (drinking while you're pregnant may affect the baby for life; a man, once divorced, usually does not come back).

I remember years ago telling my husband that there was a course I wanted to take at night. He said he'd be unhappy if I took it because it was the one evening a week he could always make it home for dinner. I had to weigh costs and benefits: the course was offered every other year. I needed it for my degree. My husband's desire to spend that one evening a week with me was also strong. I had a lot more schooling to go. He was generally supportive. These disparate pluses and minuses all went into the equation, and I weighed them against each other. I decided to take the course later, to please him and myself by choosing to spend that time with him. Had the course not been offered regularly, I might have made a different decision. But in either case, it was *me* making the decision — not out of fear of retribution by my husband or out of fear that I was being selfish. I was making a choice that I felt was right at the time. The trick isn't only to make a choice, but to give yourself freely to it — to accept the consequences of that choice. If they turn out to be unpleasant consequences, or if the choice you've made turns out to be less than ideal, you can allow yourself an error of judgment. You tried it, it didn't work, now on to something else. But preventing yourself from choosing simply because you know not everyone will be pleased is a good way to strangle the life out of yourself.

In making decisions, consider yourself *and* others. Then, having weighed the options, make the best choice you know how, one that serves *you* as much as possible. The happy dividend of making these kinds of considered choices is that, having pleased yourself, you radiate confidence and become a more positive presence in other people's lives. But even when others still aren't pleased about what you've chosen, you know you've taken the reins of your life and you can afford to be compassionate about their discomfort — even while you follow the course you know to be right.

Maturity means wholeheartedly accepting the consequences of your choices, admitting when you're wrong, but standing up for yourself when you feel you're right. No amount of obsessive people-pleasing can make you feel better than when you've done that.

Fact 5: *Some people are not capable of giving you what you're trying to get from them.*

Do I hear groans? This is another truth that hurts.

If insanity can be defined as expecting different results from doing the same thing over and over, then a lot of us have behaved crazily. We accumulate an encyclopedia of evidence that we can't get love from a parent, husband, or elusive lover — so much heartbreak and rejection and abuse — and yet still, wide-eyed and trusting, we look to them to change. We look for love in some profoundly wrong places. We can't understand it when even after saying or doing what we're convinced is exactly the right thing, the object of our attentions still doesn't change. Then we often punish ourselves for not winning that person over.

Remember my tale about meeting my father: I had to face a very painful but inescapable truth. My father, who had abandoned me as a toddler, had not magically turned into the loving daddy I'd always wanted. He could not give love because he was not equipped to give love. Looking for love from him was thus doomed from the start.

The psychological motivation for continuing to bang our heads against the same brick walls is probably familiar to you: we often try to squeeze a response out of somebody incapable of giving it to us in an attempt to master the past by recreating the original scenario — and doing everything we can to make it come out right this time. However, when a parent failed to meet our needs because of his or her own problems, we simply can't rework our history — daddy and mommy just don't have what it takes. The situation worsens when we seek stand-ins for mommy and daddy in our spouses and lovers, making a beeline for emotionally crippled people because they offer us (unconsciously) an opportunity to *make* them love us as we want to make our parents love us.

It never works.

Lisa's mother left her with an aunt when she was one year old — and then disappeared. Lisa's chances of getting a mother seemed to improve when her father remarried and took Lisa back into his house, but he'd remarried a woman who wasn't thrilled about getting a stepdaughter in the bargain. Today Lisa's stepmother would be accused of child abuse, so violent were the beatings she gave her, so neglectful was she of her needs. She felt these beatings and neglect were appropriate punishment for a misbehaving little girl. Lisa's father didn't care because he wasn't terribly aware that anything was going on: he was an alcoholic and was usually passed out by the time he'd finished dinner. But Lisa desperately wanted a mother, and so she'd get up on her stepmother's lap even at the risk of getting slapped or pushed off. As an adult, Lisa would go back to her time and time again looking for a kind word or some of the approval she'd never received as a little girl. She never got that recognition, but that didn't stop her from going back for it.

When Lisa came to see me, I suggested it might be in her best interest to seek out a surrogate mother. At first Lisa looked incredulous. She said she thought of those flannel-wrapped sticks scientists gave mother-deprived monkeys in experiments! But when I described what she might look for, she began to see what I meant: a woman she could look up to, a mentor, a teacher — someone in the community she admired, someone she'd seen and had always wanted to get to know better. Lisa saw that there were other, older women she could turn to as friends for some of the nurturing she'd never gotten before. It wasn't that she needed to turn these unsuspecting women into "mothers"; merely to seek out kind, nurturing people in an attitude of friendship. She's discovering that there are many other ways to get what she's seeking than those she'd been battling to make work all of her life. She's got choices: nurturing is available from people other than a stepmother who can't give it.

The struggle to find love where it can't be found can have some heartbreaking consequences. The victims of wife battering are often women who are compelled to choose husbands who are like their abusive fathers. Unconsciously they gravitate to the only kind of love they feel they deserve because it is the only kind of love they ever knew. For many abused women, the abuser is the only person in their lives, and even someone who beats you is better than nobody at all.

It's crucial to stop looking for emotional sustenance from people who can't give it to you. How many people are there in your life who promise but don't deliver, who are never truly there for you when you need them, who *say* they care about you but treat you indifferently, or worse? Make a mental list of the people who have disappointed you — not the occasional or accidental disappointment, but those who've chronically let you down. What traits do they have in common? Are they like your mother or father? Have you been trying to get from them what your parents never gave you?

There are no quick answers to these questions, simple as they seem to be. Our denial about the loveless people in our lives, particularly when they're part of our family, when they're our parents or spouses or even children, is very hard to break through. But if you're persistent enough in looking at your list of "disappointers" — if you make the effort to make connections, to see that you've been turning, again and again, to inappropriate people for love, security, stability, or approval — you'll start to break through that denial. You'll become clearer about the type of person who simply can't give you what you're after, and you'll begin to be able to define a new type of person who *will* be able to come through for you.

This doesn't suggest you should tear down everyone in your life. If, for example, your parents supplied you with a roof over your head, food, and clothing — even if they were short on love or other emotional support — it's healing to be grateful to them for that, to focus on what was positive in your upbringing rather than solely on what was negative, because it enables you to stop resenting and obsessing over them. If you're alive, you have the stuff to work with to start making positive changes. If there's been abuse, neglect, alcoholism, or even insanity in your family, the key is not to obsess over those negative influences, but rather to see them as warnings, as elements of your past you do not need to make part of your present. You have the power to go forward to make a nurturing environment for yourself.

Perhaps this all seems like pretty bleak sustenance compared to all those "Dick and Jane" family scenarios, or the TV families we've all seen, against which you may have measured your own family experiences. But maybe that should encourage you to explode another myth. There *is* no Dick and Jane. We all have suffered deprivation of various sorts and to varying degrees.

Most important is that regardless of who our biological parents were, unless they were able to offer us some basic, sustaining love and affection, they were not — and are not now — our *functional* parents. Some of us, in fact, haven't had functional parents at all. We were brought into the world by people who didn't have the wherewithal to parent, even if they're the people we continue to address as mother and father. We've had to look for that basic love and caring in other people and places. Sometimes we've had to become our *own* parents to get that love.

Take a long look at the needs you're still trying to meet and see if they carry over from the needs your parents couldn't fulfill for you. Are you still trying to get mom and dad, or stand-ins for mom and dad, to come up with the goods?

Only when you realize their bins have long been empty can you begin to see that there are hundreds — thousands — of other stores. You have so many more places to look for what you want than you realize.

SUGGESTED EXERCISE

If you can't seem to stop yourself from expecting love and attention from certain people, even when you rationally know they can't give it to you, try the following. Make a list of exactly what you want this person to give you — and make it as specific as possible. A sample list might be:

I want him/her to: (1) tell me I'm attractive; (2) remember my birthday; (3) ask me how my day was; (4) help me when I ask to be helped; (5) express affection.

It's important to be specific: stay away from generalities like "I want love" or "I want security"; however strong those needs may be, they're too large to tackle all at once. Now, next to each specific want you've delineated, imagine how you might fulfill it — not by trying to squeeze it out of someone who has proven he or she can't give it to you, but in different, more imaginative ways. Who are some of your friends you *can* turn to for support? What on your list might you be able to provide yourself? You can treat yourself well on your birthday, you can congratulate yourself on the triumphs of the day or console yourself when you need sympathy: don't forget the help you can be to yourself! What people *are* there for you in your life? Focus on them, and allow yourself to feel gratitude for their support. The point is to remember the range of options you have to meet your needs. If you can't get water out of a rock, then look for a stream. I guarantee there are any number of streams nearby.

Fact 6: *The way you treat yourself sets the standard for others.*

This is another truism that is more slippery than it may first appear to be. You are probably very aware of a number of women who seem to get exactly what they set themselves up to get: they walk around in unpressed clothes and wouldn't consider treating themselves to nice things. They can't be bothered to put on makeup, they stand in a slouch, they barely have the energy to get out to the supermarket, much less to pursue a job or a satisfying relationship. They eat badly, and too much. Their self-esteem is so palpably low, you don't wonder that their lives are a mess. What else would you cxpcct?

It's always easier to see the truth about other people than about yourself. You may not be hanging around in a baggy sweatshirt, you may take a bit more care with your appearance than what I've just described, but are there other ways you're holding yourself back? Ways that predict how the world will treat you — because it's all you expect of the world?

Our behaviors toward ourselves telegraphs what we expect from the people around us. When we say and do things that indicate a lack of self-respect, the message goes out loud and clear: it's okay to walk all over me, to take advantage of me, to be cruel. But when we say and do things that indicate we like ourselves, we trumpet a very different message: I'm a worthwhile person, I deserve to be treated well. And the world, you can depend on it, takes note.

I once told a woman who came to me because she felt deluged by responsibilities, swamped by bills, beyond any possibility of living the happy life she'd always hoped for herself, to go out and buy a pillow. Why a pillow? Because she also told me that one thing she'd always wanted was a beautiful bedroom, with a bed full of lacy pillows and chintz drapery. She knew exactly the bed she wanted, but she'd long ago resigned herself to the impossibility of ever getting it.

But she could start with a pillow. So she went out and bought that pillow — a lacy, extravagant pillow, which she put in the center of her plain bed. It became a symbol to her — a beacon of a better life she was getting an inkling she might be able to move toward bit by bit. Or, as it happened, pillow by pillow. Because that wasn't the last pillow she bought — she added to her collection until her bed began to transform itself. She began to transform as well. She saw herself as more deserving. She began to orchestrate her life so that she gave herself better opportunities. She awakened, slowly, to the idea that she could use her talents and intelligence and skills to better advantage. At fifty-three, she is a beautiful woman, and friends of hers suggested she'd make a terrific model. She thought that was out of the question because of her age. But as her new lacy pillows piled up, she began to gain confidence. She decided to take a risk — get a portfolio together and make the rounds of modeling agencies. To her delight, she's just signed a lucrative contract at a major agency: she was just what they were looking for!

The fact that she's a model astonishes her, but something deeper elates her. The world is now responding to her more positively than she ever thought possible. Why? Because *she* is more positive. She'd made the choice to treat herself well, and it precipitated a domino effect among the people around her.

Does this sound like a fairy story, a sentimental little

tale — "It All Began with a Pillow"? Actually, it's the result of a scientific experiment anyone can reproduce in the laboratory of her own life. Do something that shows you care about yourself, and watch the changes begin — not only in yourself, but in people who react to you.

A dividend is that taking yourself out, dressing well (which you can do within your budget), creating pleasant surroundings, and choosing to be with pleasant people conveys another clear message. You obviously don't need anyone else's opinion or approval or help: you're living a good life right now, under your own power. You're discovering you can be "more" under your own steam — you don't need someone else's approval, you don't depend on the outside world for your self-definition. This is an essential point, and it prepares us for much else we'll be discussing in this book: when you start to appreciate that you already have the resources to be a complete human being, when you trust that you have what it takes to rely on yourself, you're preparing yourself for full personhood. You won't feel the need to scramble around looking for missing pieces from outside yourself. It's not that you're already complete — none of us is all we could be — but rather that you have all the resources you need within you to move *toward* completeness.

We're all capable of this self-confidence if we allow ourselves to be. And becoming capable of it starts with realizing that we *deserve good treatment* — which we can prove by treating ourselves well! A dramatic illustration of this quickly comes to mind: I was once at a dinner party with several couples. The husband of one couple had had a little too much to drink and he began to publicly berate his wife. Instead of sitting there trying to ignore him, or making a joke of it, or in any other way trying to grin and bear it "graciously," the wife calmly stood up, turned to her hostess and thanked her for a lovely dinner and evening, and said it was time for her to leave. She then called a cab and went home.

Later, when her husband got home and began to stammer how much she'd embarrassed him, she brought him to an abrupt halt. She made it clear that his behavior was not acceptable to her and if he ever did it again, she'd respond in exactly the same way.

Could you manage that? Can you calmly tell people that you expect to be treated with courtesy and consideration — even your husband? Can you set limits and boundaries with regard to what is acceptable and unacceptable behavior? You can if you start to set those boundaries with yourself. You can if you think you deserve to be treated with respect. You will be treated with dignity when you learn to cherish the source of it: you.

SUGGESTED EXERCISE

Create for yourself your own real-life pillow story. Pick an area of your life where you feel particular dissatisfaction right now — an area in which you feel you could never change, where you feel especially stuck or inadequate. Perhaps you've always wanted to be a writer, but you feel you're not educated enough, or you don't know how to use a typewriter (much less a word processor). Make yourself go to a bookstore and look for beginning books on writing. Set aside a half hour every day to write whatever you want to — poetry, thoughts, feelings, free association. Make it your private time, and make it a *pleasure*. Give yourself permission to *play* with your thoughts, words, ideas. Sign up for a creative-writing course — or one in word-processing. Don't overwhelm yourself: limit yourself, at first, to one class a week for a circumscribed time, perhaps six weeks.

You can do the equivalent first-step work in any other area of your life. Perhaps you've always wanted to paint, meet new people, get a better job. Approach whatever your goal is as our "pillow lady" learned to: commit yourself to the first achievable small step of providing something you want for yourself. Make every subsequent step achievable too. Everything can be broken down into manageable components: even Everest is climbed one foot at a time. Prove this to yourself by taking the first manageable step — today.

Fact 7: *There are no quick fixes that can permanently change your life.*

We live in an era of fast-food mentality. We want to believe that there is a cream out there we can put on at night and wake up the next morning wrinkle-free. We cling to the hope that the next miracle diet we try will do what its advertising promises and pare off twenty pounds in a week — as we continue to feast on chocolate ice cream and pizza. We dream that our lives will be transformed by the instant magic of love, the lottery, or favorable litigation. If wishing could make it so, American women would be the richest, youngest, thinnest group of married CEOs in the world.

But — surprise! — wishing doesn't make it so. And, frankly, it's good that it doesn't. Getting something too easily deprives us of the joy of seeing our own labors add up to something. It would deprive us of growth and wisdom.

Nothing you can buy in a jar, box, or plain brown wrapper will make you look younger, trim inches off your middle, or make miraculous changes in your life all by itself. Hard-truth time again: everything worthwhile in life requires effort, commitment, and discipline. It has always been that way and always will be.

This isn't the first time you've heard this news, but don't you still resist it? Perhaps it's no wonder that we've succumbed to so many of the claims of advertising — it all sounds so good and easy and instantly doable. Unfortunately, it's lulled us and lured us so far away from the good old work ethic that few of us know what is it anymore to apply ourselves wholeheartedly to a task, to see something through to completion. We've lost touch with the thrill of challenging ourselves to achieve something extra, something beyond what we thought (or were told) we could do. I don't preach hard work because it's vaguely "good for you" — suffering for its own sake is just masochism. But a little suffering in service of something better, of something that will make your life happier and fuller — that's the kind of suffering that turns out to be worthwhile.

You can't go on a diet for a few weeks and win a lifelong struggle with obesity. You cannot exercise once a week and stay fit. You cannot peruse one book in a library for half an hour and be educated. The process of learning to accept that something worthwhile takes work doesn't, however, have to be full of grim determination. It can start with something joyful: a vision of who you want to be.

How do you develop that vision? First, by giving yourself permission to have one. It's no secret now that that's an implicit goal for us in this book: developing the self-confidence first to feel we're deserving, then to believe that we've got the resources to bring to life whatever vision we allow ourselves to have. I've put so much emphasis on breaking down goals into manageable pieces because that's how goals get achieved — by anyone. But you have to develop the goal in the first place, and keep the vision of that goal always in your mind's eye. We often turn to quick gratifications because we feel it's no use to expect anything that takes more effort. We don't feel we've got whatever that effort takes. You can turn things around (again, like our pillow lady) by focusing on the pleasure and reward of what that greater goal could mean in your life. When the vision becomes strong enough — as it will when you start to see yourself as deserving — it will guide you: you'll begin, by however small increments, to work a little harder and with more purpose, to save money, organize your life, pay off your debts, until, piece by piece, the "puzzle" of your vision begins to complete itself. Yes, it takes courage. Yes, it takes determination and hard work and discipline. But the rewards are incalculable. You won't only be on the way to achieving your goal. You'll have developed a new belief in yourself.

Again, that belief can't come out of a box, bottle, or jar. It has, as the late John Houseman used to say in commercials, to be earned. And it can be. Just keep the vision of who you want to be bright enough, and you'll do whatever you have to do to give that vision shape. How do you keep it bright? The pillow lady exercise I gave you at the end of Fact 6 can be helpful here, too: it will encourage you to believe in your goals by showing you how to achieve them. That's how you keep your vision going — and how you can allow your vision to sustain you.

Fact 8: Life is on a rheostat, not an on/off switch.

We are so used to thinking that life is all or nothing — "on" or "off." Either we're perfectly, transcendently in love or we're with the most terrible man in the world. We're either the best or the worst at what we do. Because we've turned to others for approval for so much of our lives, we have learned to rate ourselves severely — in anticipation of others rating us. Women are notoriously hard on themselves; and we're often just as demanding in what we expect of the world. We're striving so hard to please: shouldn't others strive just as hard to please us? It's that dangerous sense of entitlement we've met before — dangerous because our expectations doom us to disappointment.

Life is on a rheostat: it can glow softly brighter or dimmer. There is a whole seamless, continuous range of possibility in life. You don't have to strive for the unachievable perfect "10"; you can discover, if you allow yourself, that there's a "comfort zone" in which you can be happy. Your comfort zone will change depending on changing circumstances and age. Your goals at twenty-five may be very different from your goals at forty-five. What makes us comfortable changes as we grow — grow old *and* up.

When you decide it's all or nothing, when your standards for what you want in a man or a job or a home are so impossibly high that you either go crazy trying to achieve them or give up in defeat before you've even started, you're shortchanging yourself — badly. You're more than likely responding to somebody else's standards of success or happiness, whether your mother's or those of "Lifestyles of the Rich and Famous." What you're more than likely *not* doing is listening to yourself, your own inner voice.

Heeding your inner voice is crucial. It's what allows you to discover the range of possibilities that can make you happy. As Fact 1 showed us ("No one can bring your life to you"), depending on others to come up with magic solutions to our problems, to come up with our goals, to come up with a route to achieving those goals, is doomed from the start. What we're listening to is *somebody else's* goals. Just as if we're trying to cram feet into shoes that don't fit, we're going to be in pain. Other people's goals are exactly that: *other* people's goals. To discover what

you want means learning to listen to yourself. It's harder
to do than you may think — especially after all those
years of attuning your ears to somebody else's song.

Don't edit yourself out. Listen to all you've got to say
to yourself. Too often we chop our dreams off before we've
given them a chance to unfold, even in our imaginations.
We censor ourselves with "I'm just being silly" or "That'll
never work" or "What could I be thinking of?" I guarantee
you that whenever you hear one of those negative messages, you're *not* listening to yourself. Whom then are
you listening to?

SUGGESTED EXERCISE

Remember the maxims and messages you began to identify back in the last chapter when you told your story to
yourself? Take out pen and paper once again and make
two columns on the page. On the left, write "Messages,"
and on the right, write "From." Now, under the "Messages" heading, list some of the maxims you identified
before. "You'll never succeed." "It's a man's world." "You
can't do what you want to do." "Life means sacrificing
yourself for others." "If you risk change, you risk disaster." "All women should be married and have children."
Once you get started on your own list, it may be hard to
stop: we all have what can seem like an endless flow of
admonitions that we unconsciously broadcast to ourselves. They may all pour out when you start to make
them conscious.

Now consider each maxim and try to *hear* it in your
head.

Who's talking to you? Is the voice familiar? What does
the speaker look like? Write down the name of the speaker
next to each maxim in the "From" column. Get ready for
a formidable cast of characters. Your mother. Your father.
A grandparent. A teacher, aunt, boss, first husband. The

speakers will crowd in on you, but one thing above all will be clear: none of them is you.

The demands we make of ourselves that we *think* are ours are often very deeply internalized from demands others have made on us, usually going back to our earliest childhood. Giving yourself the meditative time to sort out those demands is essential; it's the only way to get in touch with what *you* want, not what you think you're supposed to want.

When you sort out what you want even a little bit, you may discover something amazing: certain aspects of your life may be fine right now. You can make do with certain things just as they are (even if one of your internalized outside voices berates you for being where you are), but you *can't* make do with others (even if your voices tell you that you ought to be able to). Discovering your own loves and hates is part of the task; so is discovering your likes and dislikes. Listening to yourself can mean letting up on yourself — and allowing yourself to evolve into who *you* want to be, not trying to force yourself into somebody else's image.

Fact 9: *Some problems cannot be solved, but you can make peace with them.*

Americans are brought up on the fiction that there is always a happy ending. One of our main contributions to popular culture, the sitcom, hammers this fiction home every time we turn on the television. Problems are resolved within a half hour: at the end of the show, everything is nicely tied up with a ribbon.

However, there are experiences that are wildly out of your control, that will not respond to the sitcom quick fix: When somebody you love dies. When you or someone you love becomes critically ill. When you're unexpectedly fired from your job. When your husband leaves you. When you discover your child is on drugs or that she's pregnant. These are only some of the most obvious, major disasters, but others, less dramatic but equally painful, have no doubt plagued your life. Life does not always have happy endings. Sometimes you face inescapable pain, pain that won't wash away with easy palliatives, easy moralistic platitudes. Sometimes it just *hurts*.

But how on earth are you supposed to make peace with something that hurts so much? What I mean by this "fact" is that you can contain all the experience in your life without capsizing. You can recover your balance. You can move to a plane of real understanding and acceptance of difficult circumstances, rather than plunging into a major depression because of them. Everything in life offers opportunity, if not always for hope, then for knowledge. Accepting that some of the hardships that plague us are sad but a part of life is perhaps the keystone of maturity. It allows us to shed some dangerous naïveté and develop into women of substance.

While this fact is the hardest to swallow — that life doesn't always have happy endings — it's one of the most important ones we face. It's a major test of our grown-up status. A woman named Jenny offers poignant illustration.

Jenny's son died of leukemia at the age of twelve. She had spent all of her son's short life seeking the latest medical treatments. She held out the hope that a miracle would happen and the disease would go into permanent remission, but it did not. "I didn't think I'd ever survive his death," she says today, five years later. "And a part of me hasn't survived it. I think part of me will always grieve for the life my son never had. Part of me died with him." Jenny believes that her continuing grief is appropriate. "How else can I feel?" she asks. But she has also, over time, learned to go on with her life. "I went through all the stages of grief everyone told me I would — rage, disbelief, depression, inexpressible sadness," she says, "and some other stages nobody ever warned me about. But, while I can't say it's exactly *better* today, I do realize — maybe more deeply than ever before — what a *gift* life is. How fragile, precious. Now I know that anyone's hold on life is tenuous. Including my own." Over time, Jenny has given herself permission to live — which means permission to dream, to hope, and to enjoy what she can. The experience of her son's death is, in some ways, as painful to her now as it ever was, but it has also deepened her resolve to live as fully as she can. "I now have a perspective I never had before. I've softened. I'm less judgmental. My tolerance has grown for all the mistakes we all can't help but make. Things I once thought were important just aren't anymore. I'm learning to accept people and circumstances for what they are."

This realism has led to something lasting: a new strength and balance. When I say that accepting this ninth fact allows us to become women of substance, I mean that learning to accept tragedy, or something unalterably "negative," allows us ultimately to tolerate what life gives us with more resilience and understanding than we may once have thought possible. We may, in fact, be able to do more. Jenny has now gotten involved in fund-raising for leukemia research. She speaks to various community groups about the devastation of this disease. Drawing from her own pain and experience, she has become an extraordinarily effective spokesperson. She has also added immeasurable meaning and purpose to her life.

What Jenny has developed is something called "altruistic egoism": she gives to others as she gives to herself. Jenny has transformed her pain into something she can use productively, strengthening her own sense of self in the process. You cannot truly grow up until you've made

peace with your pain — even though it may take years to
do this fully. Even if you haven't suffered the kind of
tragedy Jenny has, there are undoubtedly painful areas in
your own life you have the opportunity to face, and perhaps even to transform, so that you develop your own
sense of altruistic egoism. Pain can be an extraordinary
teacher. It can become the source of our greatest strength.

Right now, however, you may want to do nothing more
than take a deep breath. I know that swallowing all these
Facts of Life whole — in one chapter — may seem over-
whelming. But remember that these are goals as much as
facts. They constitute a grown-up perspective to spend
your life moving toward. This is the longest chapter in
the book because it maps, in a sense, the widest territory
and gives us an overview it may take you years to understand fully and incorporate into your life.

Look back at these facts from time to time as we go
ahead. Look at them as reminders of where you're going,
reminders of the climate you want to create in your life.
But now that you've taken that deep breath, let's go on
to something more immediate. It's time to turn our attention to what we can do right *now* to start making
healthy changes.

3

■■■■■■■■■■■■■■■■■

How to Stop Spinning Your Wheels and Start Living Your Life (Learning the Four Rs)

■■■■■■■■■■■■■■■■■■■

THE idea of actually *doing* something different in your life can, I know, be terrifying. You may be able to bring yourself to the point of imagining what you'd like to do next — maybe even planning for it — but actually taking steps to turn that dream and plan into reality can sometimes stop you cold. Taking my first TV job meant facing what was once a crippling phobia for me: I was terrified of flying. Not only would I have to set up a household in a new city and make new friends, but I'd have to commute weekly, by plane, to get there! It was only by learning to face my worst fear (which, of course, wasn't really a fear of flying but a fear of *crashing*) that I've been able to contain that fear and function anyway. I had a powerful motivating force: unless I got over my phobia and got on a plane, I wouldn't get the job I really wanted. Getting over that phobia, which I did by means of "implosive therapy" (which I'll explain in detail in chapter 4), meant facing it head-on. And while the fear hasn't gone away completely (with the airlines' vacillating safety records, some amount of wariness strikes me as reasonable!), the point is that I did find ways to look a terrible phobia in the face and drain it of its power. I learned that my fears don't have to control me.

Your fears don't have to control you, either.

You may have come to this book because change seems like a hurdle you've never felt capable of clearing. So far I've given you some general guidelines for reclaiming your life — for depending on yourself for direction rather than on the pushes and prods of other people. You probably identify with the problems those guidelines address. By now, you can see that our major obstacle is fear: the insecurity so many of us feel has deep roots, some of them societal, some of them peculiar to our own upbringing and psychology.

But, again, I promise that you can face that fear and surmount it. You have the power to change your life: after twenty-three years of practice, in which I've seen thousands of women face and conquer all kinds of fear, I have no doubts about this. The willingness to change your life does involve courage; there's no getting around that. But if you've read this far, you've already demonstrated enough courage and willingness to go forward. To begin, all I want you to do is to open the door a crack. As I hope I've made clear, nobody expects you to transform your life overnight. But you can start transforming some of your attitudes right now.

As we've seen, it's our attitudes that have held us back — unquestioned assumptions about our competence, about happiness and direction and love coming from outside ourselves rather than from within. Fortunately, there's a very effective method for changing destructive attitudes, a process that starts with self-examination but ends in real change, in taking appropriate actions to begin making your life better and more satisfying. The bulk of this chapter will be devoted to this process.

But first, let's focus a little more clearly on the willingness we must feel before we can take action. I've prefaced a number of truths in this book with the word *hard* and suggested that the process of growing up, especially for women who have been taught to resist that process, consists largely of facing a number of hard truths. In over twenty years as a therapist, I've come to see that although problems come in all sizes, shapes, and varieties, there are really only two kinds of clients: those who want to change and do, and those who may want to talk about change.

Women in the first group feel provoked to make changes for a variety of reasons. Often the woman who makes rapid, dramatic changes in her life does so as a result of a catalytic event — her youngest child leaves home, she loses her job, her husband or lover walks out, someone she is close to becomes ill or dies. Or she may be motivated by a sudden insight, in which all at once she sees herself and her life with crystal clarity and says, in effect, "My God, I've been putting myself through this for twenty years and I'm not going to do it anymore." She's often the person who looks at the drink in her hand, or the cigarette, or the man who's been abusing her and just quits cold turkey (hopefully, however, with some follow-up therapy). You may be in that group of women who just announce, "Today is the beginning of my future" and then follow through. If so, even though you may sometimes fall back and have to start anew, count yourself lucky. You already have a strong willingness to change and will more than likely be receptive to taking the right action to make your life better.

The dissatisfaction you feel with your life may not be quite so dramatic, however. You may feel a lingering, generalized depression or anxiety — knowing something is wrong but not quite being able to put your finger on what it is. Perhaps something of what you've read in the first two chapters has helped to nudge you into greater clarity; you may feel that the feminine mistake of not allowing yourself to direct your own life comes closest to defining your problem. If so, fine! That's as specific as you need to be at this point to go further. Concrete actions to make your life more fulfilling will occur to you if you'll just allow yourself to be open enough now to take the first steps you'll learn in this chapter.

However, if you're a woman who has taken refuge in her problems — who gets pleasure out of complaining that she "can't" accomplish more, be stronger and more assertive, control her temper or her eating or her "addictions" to certain men — the process I'm offering will be more difficult. The whole notion of blaming what's wrong in your life on men or behavior you "just can't control" needs to be rethought — and released. In fact, the whole notion of blaming anything or anyone — even yourself — is unproductive. Alas, it's not uncommon for a woman to fall into this trap, feeding masochistically on the "certainty" that she's inadequate, or on the meager pleasure of pointing her finger at the "real problem": the man or the family or the lack of money that's allegedly holding her back. As we've already seen, this blame-mongering does nothing but keep us exactly where we are. To change positively, we have to allow the attitude that it's "all their fault" or "it's all too much" to change.

Most "can'ts" are really "won'ts." When you say you can't meet new people because you're too tired after a full day's work; you can't travel because you couldn't imagine going anywhere by yourself; you can't take a computer course because you haven't been able to find a baby-sitter; you can't lose weight because there's always ice cream in the refrigerator and you have to buy it because the family wants it — when you say any of these things, what you're really admitting is that you won't take action to change things. I don't say this to berate you: none of us has entirely escaped the "can'ts." And it may be, for example, that you really want to eat ice cream more than you want to lose weight, but you just haven't acknowledged it to yourself. The goal is to wake up to the reality of your true wants — to accept responsibility for your own actions, not to blame your lack of success on circumstances "beyond control." All of us have the power to see when "can't" really means "won't" and accept the responsibility this implies. If you admit to yourself that you don't want to stop eating sweets, you've at least accepted responsibility for your actions; you have decided that the cost of slimness is too high. If, however, you hate being heavy — you feel you are destroying your health by eating badly and too much, and you dearly wish you were slimmer — you are in a position to make appropriate positive change. You have already accepted responsibility for your eating habits, which means you know that you have the power to change them.

Changing "can't" to "can" only happens when you see it's really a question of changing "won't" to "will." The following program for change — what I call the Four Rs — will, I think, help you see this for yourself.

■■■■■■■■■■■■■■

The Four Rs

The Four Rs of positive change are:

- Recognition
- Realization
- Reassessment
- Re-creation

Look at the first and final Rs and you'll see where the process begins and where it's designed to end: from thought to creation. In a nutshell, that's how any change occurs. You get the idea, you consider how to bring it to reality, then you take steps to make it reality. Perhaps this seems simple, even obvious. However, how many times have you or others you have known jumped into action without thought? You take the first job offered you out of fear that you will never be offered another job; you marry the first man who asks you out of similar panic; you buy a dress or a rug or a house on impulse and only when it's too late discover that the dress does not flatter you, the carpet is not stain-resistant, and the house needs major plumbing and electrical work.

The way to guard against these impulses, these actions taken out of fear or anxiety, is to give yourself time to see what you're doing before you do it. This means applying the first R of the four I've presented:

1. Recognition

Recognizing a problem is the first step to solving it — as a client of mine, Claire, will help me to illustrate. She came to therapy with a number of complaints, the major one physical: she suffered from debilitating, excruciatingly painful headaches. All previous medical attempts to help her had failed.

In discussing her background with her, I learned that ever since she was a little girl, she had taken care of her younger sister, Marian. Their mother had died early in their childhood, and Claire had always felt the obligation to take over Marian's mothering. By now, even though they were both adults, it had become second nature for Claire to worry about Marian and give in to Marian's every whim — a situation that Marian had learned to exploit.

For example, Marian had never learned to drive, largely because she could always depend on Claire to drive her wherever she wanted to go. Although Marian had a husband and, by this time, a grown daughter, both of whom drove, she said she didn't want to impose on them to take her on errands. Somehow it had never seemed like an imposition to depend on Claire — all their lives, Claire hadn't minded doing anything Marian asked, so why would it be a problem now?

In fact, Claire was starting to mind a great deal, although she hadn't allowed herself to acknowledge it. Her resentment was intensifying, even though she wasn't at first aware of its roots. Her buried anger manifested itself in terrible headaches and huge sweeping moods of depression, which led Claire into therapy. Even the pain clinic Claire sought as a last resort couldn't help her. She was at her wits' end.

I asked Claire when these headaches typically hit her; in almost every case it was right after Marian called to ask "one more favor" — to be picked up and taken on yet another errand. While the connection to Marian was clear to me, it wasn't clear to Claire at all. She couldn't allow herself to acknowledge her resentment because it would have triggered massive guilt; it would have meant she wasn't taking care of Marian the way she'd always felt she was supposed to. Then I asked Claire what she thought was the worst that could happen if she ever said no to Marian. Claire looked fearful for a moment. "Why, she'd — she'd — call me selfish! She'd say I didn't love her. She'd complain about me to the rest of the family!" Obviously, these were terrifying possibilities to Claire. I asked her to consider even more specifically what these worst-case scenarios would entail — would they be so bad? "Try to visualize them," I said, "and practice how you would deal with each."

Claire considered them one by one, imagining how Marian might really react to the news that Claire no longer wanted to chauffeur her to the grocery store, the doctor, the post office. She began to see that it was obvious from their past that she'd demonstrated her love for her sister many times over — and that she had never set limits on what was reasonable or appropriate for Marian to expect. She began, in other words, to recognize what the real problem was. The real problem wasn't that Marian kept wanting Claire to drive her everywhere; it wasn't even that Marian was insensitive and demanding. The real problem was that Claire thought she had to prove her selflessness and love to her sister by always saying yes to her requests. The real problem was that Claire had never learned to set limits with Marian, to let Marian know that Claire had needs too, that she wasn't a chauffeur or a doormat. She had to stop blaming Marian — Marian quite honestly didn't know Claire was unhappy, because Claire had never expressed her unhappiness.

The hard truth Claire had to face was that most people want their own needs met, and they'll go to great lengths to see that they're met, sometimes at the expense of other people's needs — especially when those other people don't appear to mind being exploited. People can't read your mind about what you want: you have to tell them when you feel you're being ignored or mistreated.

Recognizing the real problem is not, as you can see from Claire's example, always so easy. Claire had been conditioned to feel guilty for so long that she was afraid to take a deep look at her own feelings — she was afraid to acknowledge that she felt used and stepped on. She had to make a leap of courage to admit to herself that she felt Marian was violating some important boundaries.

Only then could she be in a position to make those boundaries explicit, to let Marian know she couldn't always be at her beck and call. Once Claire had this recognition she was ready to go one step farther: she was ready to face the next R in our plan:

2. Realization

Once you've recognized the problem, you need to do what Claire did: make connections. See what the problem indicates about you and about what may be holding you back, not just in the specific instance you've been able to pinpoint, but in other areas of your life as well. Once Claire realized that her headaches and depression stemmed from feelings of duty to her sister, she began to realize what some of the assumptions were that underlay feeling dutiful — assumptions that, she could see, were holding her back in far more than just her relationship with Marian. She'd grown up feeling she had to take care of everyone. Her role in life was to be "the little mother," so that her own mother could "look down from heaven" and approve of her, be proud of her. Unfortunately, this did not prove to be sufficient reward. As Claire grew older, her resentment at being trapped by "the little mother" role deepened, even though she could not express that resentment directly — it came out in the form of excruciating headaches. No one wants to be trapped by others' expectations, and unconsciously we almost always manifest rebellion, either by becoming physically ill or withdrawing emotionally or blowing up. Our psyches know that we have trapped ourselves even when our conscious minds do not! And our bodies and emotions follow suit: as in Claire's case, they send out warning signals — headaches, fatigue, chest pain, or any number of other symptoms.

Our second R — realization — is crucial, because it

brings us to a deeper appreciation of what's really holding us back. While we need to see and acknowledge — or recognize — the symptoms of our unhappiness and label their cause as clearly as we can, we also need to see what these symptoms are really saying about us, what the problem may be underneath those symptoms. Once Claire made the connection that she'd been living her life out of duty, out of the assumption that she had to prove her devotion to her sister to get her dead mother's approval, she had a revelation that helped her in all areas of her life. She was able to see other ways in which she responded reflexively to people — to her friends as well as to her sister. Claire was always the one who volunteered to bring the food to get-togethers, she was always the one who volunteered to clean up afterward: "I don't mind!" could have been her motto. She'd turned herself into a doormat in most of her relationships. As for men, she never gave herself time or permission to meet any. She had too many responsibilities. Undergoing the second R, however, she allowed herself to realize that many of those responsibilities were really burdens of her own making, that, in many ways, they protected her from having to deal with men. She feared marriage — a fear connected to imagining that once again she'd have to be someone's total caretaker. But now, in this new state of realization, she understood that her assumptions were making her react to people in this way — and that she had the power to change those assumptions to something more positive.

This led her to the third R of our plan, where she could truly allow herself to develop a new view of possibilities, to see alternatives she never dreamed she'd be able to see. She was ready to make a:

3. Reassessment

Once you've given yourself the facts by recognizing the symptoms and realizing some of the symptoms' causes, you can now take an inventory to see how the fears beneath your choices have shaped your life. Claire was able to do this once she made a list of the ways in which she was sabotaging herself by reacting to others' requests as if they were commandments — commandments she felt compelled to follow because she once was sure she'd suffer rejection or loss of self-esteem if she didn't. She made two columns on a piece of paper, labeling one "What I Usually Do" and the other "What I Could Do Instead." They ran as follows:

What I Usually Do	*What I Could Do Instead*
Take my sister to the supermarket whenever she requests it	Suggest she call in an order and have it delivered, or take her only when I'm doing my own marketing
Take my sister to the doctor even when it conflicts with my work schedule	Suggest she arrange a ride with a nonworking friend, or offer to drop her off and have her husband or daughter pick her up
Clean up after church supper	Initiate a sign-up list of volunteers; if no one signs up, suggest paper plates and cups and plastic utensils to make clean-up easier
Stay home on Saturday nights	Plan an activity with someone I enjoy being with

Claire's list went on a good deal longer than the entries I've listed here, but you can see even from this brief roundup why the list was a revelation to her: there was so much she could change! None of the changes on her list was radical; the important point was that there were numerous small changes she could make in every area of her life to show her that she didn't have to live under so many burdens — to show her that she could delegate responsibility and ask for help from other people without being rejected or being accused of selfishness. As insignificant as these changes may appear, they had an enormous impact on her life.

It is important to stress that Claire actually wrote down this list — she didn't simply make a mental note of it. The list was to remind herself, in concrete terms she could actually read, how much power she had to change her life. She didn't have to accomplish these changes all at once; she gave herself permission to institute them gradually, practicing setting new limits in her life, one step at a time.

It amazed Claire to see how many alternatives to anger-provoking tasks she had! It's not that the new alternatives didn't themselves require "responsibility": she would have to tell her sister Marian that she couldn't jump on demand anymore and be strong enough not to plead for understanding. Making herself available to new experiences and people would mean feeling vulnerable in ways she had never allowed herself to feel before. But she would learn the risk was worth it when she accomplished the fourth R in our program:

4. Re-creation

I love the double meaning of the word *recreation:* in one sense it means to have fun, take a break from the usual grind, please yourself, while in a literal sense it means to create anew, to bring something new into being. I'd like you to think of the word in both these positive ways. When you re-create your life, you bring new pleasure and satisfaction and meaning to it, you don't simply change it for the sake of changing it. Arbitrary change, as we discussed earlier, cannot bring lasting happiness because it is not done in response to your real desires. You may want to change everything and perhaps have even given in to the impulse to do so unthinkingly, but more than likely you simply repeated all of the "mistakes" you made before, and life was no better, no matter that you changed men, jobs, or cities. Since you brought your old self to a new situation, you probably quickly re-created the same old problems — you were more than likely stuck in the same old ruts all over again.

Re-creating your life positively means changing it consciously, with as much awareness as possible of why you're making changes and what you want those changes to bring about. True re-creation begins on the inside and only then manifests itself on the outside. You've seen that Claire had to recognize what was really holding her back; realize how her fears were affecting all of her life, not just the specific instance that first made her aware of them; and then reassess what she might do to change things. Each of our first three Rs has to do with making inner changes. Only after you've attended to the inside are you ready for the work of changing the outside.

In Claire's case, the work of re-creating her life meant trying out alternatives to old behavior she knew was holding her back. It was a process of trial and error. "I'd never stood up for myself before," she said, "and the first time I said no to my sister I was choked with fear. I was sure she'd break into a tirade about how selfish I was being." Marian surprised her. She was a little shocked, but she seemed to recover remarkably quickly. "I guess I'll ask my daughter," she said — and that was that. Claire realized she had projected her sister's rejection and was living in fear of something she'd made up herself. This isn't to say it couldn't have been worse — Marian may well have made a scene or accused Claire of selfishness. And Claire would have had to learn to stand up even to this, her worst fears coming true. But as it happened (and as it so often happens), her worst fears didn't materialize. "Marian's reaction was so nonthreatening, it made me wonder how much else I was projecting on others," she said. Slowly, behavior by behavior, she tried new ways of dealing with her surroundings, being careful to give herself time for re-creation, seeing the changes as play, an adventure, not allowing her fears to get ahead of her. She slowly went down the list she'd written and actually tried each alternative, one at a time. At first it felt awkward to be good to herself. "I couldn't help feeling guilty — it just happened, like a reflex. Then I realized I had no reason to feel guilty! I could take a bath in the afternoon if I wanted to; no one was going to get mad at me or tell me I couldn't. I could arrange my weekends so that I did something I wanted to do — see a movie in the afternoon, even go out for a nice meal in a restaurant alone. I didn't have to build my life around the wants and needs of a half dozen other people. It's a slow process, learning to be good to myself, but it's wonderful. It's a real triumph when I've decided what I want to do and what I don't." Claire has also discovered that she's freed herself to enjoy doing things for other people, too: "I help people now because I want to, not because I think I have to. I'm not so resentful anymore." She's experienced another happy dividend. Her headaches have gone away.

I hope Claire's example has already suggested ways in which you might emulate her passage through the Four Rs. Here are some specific exercises that will help you, right now, to do for yourself what Claire did for herself: break out of the destructive rut of negative behavior.

■ ■ ■ ■ ■ ■ ■ ■ ■ ■ ■ ■ ■ ■

Applying the Four Rs to You — Right Now

1. RECOGNITION EXERCISE

Focus on your biggest resentment, what really makes you angry about someone else's behavior right now. Perhaps it's your mother nagging you to get married. Perhaps, if you *are* married, an in-law nags at you for not taking care of your husband or children well enough. Perhaps it's a job-related resentment: your boss or a coworker is giving you a hard time.

Once you've identified the resentment, ask yourself the following questions:

1. How much of what this person says is "wrong with me" is true? Am I willing to change this part of my behavior?

2. What part of this person's behavior toward me is unfair?

When you've identified the "unfair" component, put yourself through the following imaginary scenario: If, for example, you have a gripe about your boss giving you too much work, imagine telling him or her exactly what you perceive the problem to be — *as it affects you.* Do not focus on blaming your boss: merely state, as clearly as you can, why you feel you can't do what you're being asked to do. Now imagine the boss questioning your reasoning. Play the devil's advocate and argue (along with your boss) against yourself. Respond again, this time taking these objections into account. State the injustice, as it affects you, in even clearer terms. Keep the dialogue going until you've defined, to your complete satisfaction, what the problem is, and what the immediate reasons for it are.

2. REALIZATION EXERCISE

Focusing on the same resentment, ask yourself the following questions:

1. What part, if any, have I taken in allowing this injustice to be done to me — or to continue?

2. Are there other resentments I feel in my life that I similarly have had a part in creating or sustaining?

3. When is the first time I can remember getting into this kind of "unjust" situation?

Answering these questions as honestly as you can will enable you to begin to see a pattern of behavior by which you may have unwittingly sabotaged yourself.

3. REASSESSMENT EXERCISE

Do exactly what Claire did when she began to look at the way she had allowed her sister to exploit her. Focusing on the same resentment you've begun to explore in the first two exercises, set up two columns on a piece of paper, one labeled "What I Usually Do," the other, "What I Could Do Instead."

Now, point by point, give yourself time to imagine how you might ease or eradicate the injustice you're suffering. In the "boss/too much work" example, you might offer such alternatives as "Come up with a plan for lightening work load by spreading it more evenly in the department," "Suggest ways to improve efficiency," "Ask that title and salary be improved if work load cannot be lessened" — up to and including "Decide if situation is intolerable, and if it is, begin search for new job." Give yourself specific, workable alternatives to your old pattern of response.

4. RE-CREATION EXERCISE

Focus on the imaginary conversation you had with your "antagonist" in the first exercise so that you can remind yourself of how you've defined the problem as it relates to you. Then, pick one — the most plausible — alternative from the list you just gave yourself in the third exercise, and make a pact with yourself to bring it up with your antagonist the next time you can. If you meet with resistance, ask that you both think further about it, ask for any suggestions the other person might be able to come up with, and set an appointment to meet later to continue the discussion. In the interim, prepare the rest of your alternative solutions so that you'll be ready with more than a general complaint. But celebrate — that night or day — the fact that you've begun to break your old pattern of behavior. If your antagonist's response was positive, you'll have additional reason to celebrate, but either way, congratulate yourself in some tangible way for the triumph of starting to turn things around. Take yourself out to dinner; enjoy a bubble bath; see a movie; share your good news with a friend. You're on the way to changing your life — not by reacting blindly in the same old ways, but by *responding* with forethought, self-compassion, and positive purpose.

Recognize. Realize. Reassess. Re-create. Do you see the logic of the progression? And do you now see how you might apply this progression in your own life? I don't want to gloss over the difficulties. When you face something as entrenched as your own assumptions about what you should or shouldn't be doing, you're facing beliefs that have taken a lifetime to form. That's why giving yourself time to see, analyze, rethink, and then take action to change things is so important. You have to convince yourself of the feasibility of change before change is possible — or certainly before it will be of any lasting value. That doesn't mean there's no risk involved — there will always be risk. But the rewards of taking risks far outweigh staying in the same miserable, unhappy place. What if you end up making a mistake? You'll have learned something from the process of challenging yourself. It will help you to choose more wisely in the future; risking change is wonderful schooling. Review the Facts of Life you learned in chapter 2. Read them over for inspiration and understanding before you take the risk of changing something in your life. Remember that you can survive rejection and that you can repair or at least rebound from mistakes. Recall that happiness is possible when you reach out for it; it won't come if all you do is sit around and wait for it. Every Fact we delineated in chapter 2 applies to the process of following the Four Rs to improve your life. So refresh your knowledge of them now or whenever you need to.

You've seen from how Claire applied the Four Rs that they're not only useful for the big decisions in your life; you can make them part of your daily life to great advantage. The point is to realize that you always have access to a wonderful instrument — an instrument that you can call upon to help you assess with amazing insight and precision any situation in which you find yourself, and to help you to make sound, intelligent choices. What is this marvelous instrument?

Your mind. It can enable you to deal with any conflict in your life more innovatively than you probably realize.

Your mind is a phenomenal resource. Perhaps you'll awaken to what a wonderful machine is at your disposal if we liken it to another similar, wonderful machine: the computer.

■ ■ ■ ■ ■ ■ ■ ■ ■ ■ ■ ■ ■ ■ ■

Programming Your Daily Mind Computer

You may already know how to use a computer or a word processor. If you don't, don't worry: we won't get technical here. The analogy I'm making is accessible to anyone, computer-savvy or not. I'd simply like you to think of each new day as a new file in the computer of your mind.

One of the wonderful things about a computer is that it enables you to review data without emotional judgment; you can call up information that may at first have baffled or distressed you later on, when you feel calmer and have the time to give it your full, more objective understanding. You can use your mind in exactly the same way.

When you think of each new day as a new page in your mind's computer, you allow yourself not only to approach the present moment without the taint of the past, but to review whatever you feel you need to review about what you've been through the day before. Some people like to take this inventory at the end of a day, before going to bed. Many people find it better to store the day's events, particularly if they've been hurtful or troublesome, for review the next morning — or whenever in the future they have the time and serenity to look at them. Whichever time of day you use for this inventory or review, call up the day's events, as you would on a computer, and look at them as calmly as possible. Ask yourself some questions: What made me uncomfortable? Why? Was my ego threatened — did I feel somebody was trying to put me down? If so, how seriously do I have to take what was said? Was there any truth in it? Or did I overreact?

What made me feel good about myself on this day? Did

I say what I meant — did I make every attempt to be honest about my feelings and thoughts? Did I help anyone else in any way? Was I good to myself?

You might apply the first three Rs to the data you call up: *recognize* the problems, attempt to *realize* what may have given rise to them or what they may be concealing, and then *reassess* their importance and consider alternative ways to deal with them if they come up again. Without obsessing, attempt to write the dialogue between you and someone with whom you had a hard time communicating so that you're clearer about what both of you were trying to say.

Many conflicted clients of mine have tried this technique with wonderful results. It's a technique that keeps problem-solving in the present. Jane offers a good example. Married to Chuck, whom she loves but whom she describes quite openly as vain — "He's got an insatiable need for praise," Jane says — she sometimes feels provoked by his attempts to make her jealous. "Once he told me that he gets more attention from his secretary than he gets from me," says Jane. She grew weary and — she admits — jealous of Chuck's constant praise for his perfect secretary, Loretta. She finally lashed out, "Why don't you just have an affair with her then? Or maybe you are already! Is that why you keep talking about her? I don't know why you bother to come home to me at all." In her anger and hurt, Jane remembers telling Chuck to pick up a hot plate and move into his office — he could sleep on his couch. "Why not just move in there, and get all the attention you want from your little fan?" Chuck responded just as impulsively: "Maybe that's not a bad idea!" and stormed out of the house.

The next morning, Jane realized that Chuck had slept on the couch in their living room — some bedding was hastily folded up on the chair next to it — but that he'd left early to go to work without saying goodbye and was probably going to come home late, too. In the calmer light of a new day, Jane realized she had to deal with this as rationally as she knew how. She needed to use her mind as a computer.

She called up the previous day's dialogue between her husband and herself. She looked at it with more detachment than she could have done before. What was really going on? She brought herself through the first three Rs: *recognition* — what is the real problem? "He's making me jealous," was Jane's reply; *realization* — what underlies this feeling? "Part of me knows that what he's saying is true: I'm not paying much attention to him these days. I'm tired, busy with the kids and my job, and I don't feel very available"; *reassessment* — what are my options? "I could hire help; I could quit my job; or, at the very least, I could talk to him to let him know my real feelings."

Before Jane could get to a satisfying fourth R, *recreation*, she knew she had to talk to Chuck — that the option of talking to him to let him know her real feelings was the one she wanted to take first. And so she prepared by rewriting their dialogue to reveal what she really needed to say — and what she could imagine was beneath Chuck's own impulsive language. Here's how it ran:

JANE: It hurts me when you use other women to get attention from me.

CHUCK: You know I need a lot of attention. This woman at work understands what I'm doing, and I like the feedback she gives me.

JANE: But when you talk about her, I feel you are shutting me out and saying someone else is more important to you than I am.

CHUCK: I know I've been blocking you out, but you always seem so busy and you're never interested in what I'm doing. You're not even interested in making love anymore.

JANE: Chuck, I'm exhausted. There are not enough

hours in the day. When I get home from work I don't know what to do first. I don't want us to hurt each other. I love you and I'm jealous that you find someone else attractive. Help me find more time for us to be together and listen to each other.

Jane wasn't attempting to write an Oscar-worthy screenplay. Nor was this a conversation that could have been predicted. What she was doing for herself was simply this: getting at the real messages she was trying to convey to her husband, and attempting to understand what Chuck might have been trying to tell her. At the same time, it was also a rehearsal, an attempt to find some more effective ways of expressing what she really felt so that she could communicate better with Chuck in the future. But it was primarily a process that could enable her to disengage enough emotionally to gain perspective and strength — to express her anger or hurt in carefully considered words, not in an unthinking, emotional way.

That's the point of the computer analogy. When you give yourself time to call up even the most distressing events or feelings of the day and look at them, as far as possible, as data to be assessed, you give yourself a gift of clarity — clarity that can help you to choose your next course of action as wisely as you can. If Jane had allowed herself to stew or obsess over the hurt she felt Chuck caused her, by the time they next met she'd be even less rational than they both had been before. Giving herself time out to play the whole scenario on the screen of her mind's computer allows her to see what her present feelings are — and gives her the resources to act as she truly wants to act when she next sees Chuck. Most of all, "computerizing" her feelings and their dialogue helps her to avoid needless recriminations. Recriminations alienate; the truth, expressed with caring and respect, can help to unite.

Remember that you've got the most miraculous computer ever devised sitting right on your own shoulders: IBM still can't compete with its intricacies, its extraordinary abilities. The exciting news is that you can use your human computer far more efficiently than you may ever have realized. You can, as I've suggested, store highly charged material in it for calling up the next day. Then, when you call it up, you can choose among any number of alternatives, from "Erase" (if you decide the material isn't important enough to store) to "Recall" (if you link this information to some related thing from the past) to "Modify" (if this information alters your previous views) to "Review" (if you want to consider it when you're less emotional). The important point is that you don't have to react right away. Consider it a rule of thumb that if you're swayed by any strong, sweeping emotion — especially anger — it is not the right time to react. Remember you can always say, "I don't think this is the best time to discuss this. Let me think about it. Let's wait until we've both cooled down." That's one way of storing highly charged material for later.

Learning to store it for later helps us do something besides make us use our "computers": we're also exercising the muscle of restraint. We're increasing what psychologist Albert Ellis calls our frustration tolerance — and countering what Ellis calls the human tendency to catastrophize. Practicing restraint is perhaps the single most important lesson our "computers" have to teach us. When we keep from reacting impulsively, we give ourselves space to choose from many more options in the future, when our hot heads have cooled off.

■■■■■■■■■■■■■■

Keeping a Journal

Storing material mentally isn't your only option, however. You an also store it on paper, in a journal. Journals are wonderful tools: they can not only give you a record of the previous day's events to review in the cooler light of today or tomorrow, but over the long haul they can reveal patterns of behavior that may not be clear to you from moment to moment. Jane began to keep a journal and was amazed, a month or two down the line, to see how many times she barked not only at her husband but at friends, coworkers, and her children. She saw that every time she lost her temper she was really feeling hurt and misunderstood. She began to see the urge to blow up as a sign that something deeper wasn't being addressed — and this gave her the strength to hold back until she could find a more appropriate and helpful way of expressing her pain. The record she depended on was her journal, which has now become her most useful tool in carrying out the Four Rs.

You can keep a journal, too. In fact, the written exercises I've suggested throughout this book can comprise its beginning — it can start with the retelling of your life and move through the self-questioning you've begun to do in this and the last chapter. What these exercises are exercising is your ability to see yourself, and the possibilities of your life, in a new light. As we've seen, that's the only way you can begin to clean the slate for real change.

Make your journal comfortable to use. A loose-leaf binder is a good idea, because it will invite you to put in newspaper clippings, photographs, or any other memento or "signal" that has particular meaning to you. (Some binders have pockets for these kinds of additions, or you can simply tape whatever you'd like to add onto looseleaf paper.) Make a habit of using your journal daily, either at the beginning of the day or at the end of it, whichever feels best to you. Write down imaginary dialogues, as I've suggested doing in the Four Rs exercises, or as Jane did when she "programmed her computer." Think of your journal as a safe place, a place where anything goes. This is your own private world. Enter it and make it home. It will help you to clarify your dreams, monitor your progress toward making those dreams a reality, and simply give you space to be yourself with no fear of an audience. The book you create, over time, will be a mirror on so many levels.

Dag Hammarskjöld once said, "Read the book your life is writing." That's what I'd like you to do, too, daily, by reviewing the day's events in light of our Four Rs and, I hope, by keeping a journal to help you plot your course. Our lives give us so much information about ourselves, but information isn't helpful unless it's heeded.

What all of this is meant to give you is clarity, not only about the events in your life, but about the motives behind those events — and about your own possible role in causing those events. You'll have stopped spinning your wheels when you stop looking outside yourself and begin to see what you are doing to hold yourself back. Allowing yourself the time to think and reassess is crucial preparation for making actual change. Think of change as the fruit, the final product, of a process that begins gently and accessibly with thought. Begin by recognizing the pain, try to realize its underlying cause, and then reassess what options are available to you. You'll eventually be able to accomplish the wonderful act of re-creation; you'll be able to open the present of your life, as I promised you earlier on.

Keeping a journal can help you keep track of what's

actually going on in your life in some surprising ways. Not the least of what you'll learn is the state of your "emotional fitness" — a state that you can improve just as readily as you can your physical fitness. Remember what I said about exercising the muscle of restraint? That's only the beginning of the course you'll learn about next — a course in emotional fitness that will ensure that you won't be capsized by any changes you initiate in your life or by circumstances that hit you unpredictably.

4

················

Working Out: A Short Course in Emotional Fitness

▪▪▪▪▪▪▪▪▪▪▪▪▪▪▪▪▪▪▪▪▪▪

IF you exercise regularly, if you know what it is to have a good workout, you know that effective exercise is hard work. It takes time. You sweat. You get stronger and fitter only by challenging yourself beyond what's comfortable. And the reward? You feel great when you're through. You may or may not like the actual experience of physical exertion, but its results are undeniable: increased flexibility, balance, strength, endurance, and control.

When we face our emotions, however, suddenly our expectations change. We feel, somehow, that they're a whole different part of us — that we simply don't have the control over our emotional selves that we do over our physical selves. We wouldn't think of working out emotionally — what could that mean? We think that emotions are like unpredictable weather: we're powerless over them, and the best we can do is hope we weather the storm.

This is, unfortunately, common thinking for many

women. What many of us don't realize is that we need just as much flexibility, balance, strength, endurance, and control in our emotional lives as we do in our physical bodies. As you'll learn in this chapter, you can acquire these traits emotionally: they are in fact what constitute "emotional fitness." And when you see the results of acquiring this kind of fitness, you'll want to put yourself through a stringent "emotional workout" every day.

Making it stringent is important. As with physical exercise, if you don't challenge yourself beyond what is easy, you won't grow — it's as simple as that. And challenging yourself emotionally is in many ways a lot harder — and sometimes a lot more frightening — than doing an extra two laps in the pool or an extra mile of walking or jogging. Challenging yourself emotionally means facing your worst fears head-on.

It's amazing what you can learn when you pass through that fear.

■■■■■■■■■■■■■■■

Fourteen Women in Colorado

I recently spent a weekend in Aspen, Colorado, with thirteen other women. Two were friends of mine, the rest I didn't know. But at the end of three days, there were no strangers in the group. We felt as bonded to each other as if we'd known each other all our lives.

The idea of the weekend was simply this: we got together with the express purpose of facing our fears. I have known for many years the wonderful rewards of getting past fear, but I knew that I was still held back by certain fears, mostly the fear of loss of control. I knew it was time for a "workout" to get over more of it. As I mentioned at the beginning of the last chapter, I once had a terrible phobia about flying — a phobia that, had I let it control me, would quite simply have prevented me from following the career I have today. Flying was agony to me, until I put myself through an emotional workout called "implosive therapy," a process in which I imagined, in full, unedited detail, going through the experience I dreaded most: *crashing*. I sweated, I clenched, I went through every worst-case scenario my vivid imagination could paint — I spared myself nothing. I came out of it like a dishrag, but I came out of it. I had allowed myself to undergo something that I never thought I could face — and I found that I could. It was a catharsis. I found I could get on a plane without breaking into a cold sweat. I had come through.

But my newfound resilience was severely tested a couple of years ago. I was on the runway in a plane about to take off from Detroit for Los Angeles — my weekly commute — when the ill-fated Northwest flight crashed immediately after takeoff, killing all but one on board — one of the worst airline disasters in the history of aviation. Our plane taxied back to the airport, and we got off while the wreckage — the wreckage that could have been my plane — was dealt with. I was white with fear; it all came back. But even in the midst of my panic, I knew I had to get back on that plane. I felt strongly that if I didn't, I'd never get on another in my life. I managed to pass through fear once again and reboard. In many ways, that was the most important flight I've taken in my life.

This is only one example of passing through fear. The women with whom I shared my Colorado weekend had many fears of their own. In fact, sharing our fears was part of our goal. We each came to this weekend with the goal of facing — and getting through — one fear that especially terrified us. We each came to this weekend with the goal of challenging ourselves to see what we'd find, to see how far we could go beyond what we'd ever done before.

One woman feared groups. She hated having to be

around other people and was afraid of intimacy of any kind. Simply being with this many other women whom she didn't know was a test in itself.

Another woman had a very private fear, one she did not reveal until the weekend was over, and then only to two of us: a spot had been found on her brain and she faced the likelihood of brain surgery. She was terrified at the possible consequences, choked with fear of the unknown.

There was also a young widow whose husband had died horribly in a motorcycle crash ten years before, leaving her, in her early twenties, to bring up their child alone. The past ten years had already been a test of fear, but now she faced the prospect of a new marriage, and she was terrified of it. She didn't want to risk loving another man whom she might also lose.

Another woman identified her worst fear as the fear of isolation. She was terrified of being alone. Then she revealed that she'd spent her adult life working first as an archaeologist in Egypt — painstaking work, most of it done solo — and subsequently with dolphins in this country. I suggested that her real fear was of intimacy — her work was virtually designed to keep her away from other human beings. A light went on in her eyes: she realized that her fear of intimacy was what she'd really come to work on.

Still another woman, married for twenty-five years to a man who had dominated her physically and emotionally, now, after her divorce, found herself getting involved with men who were less educated, less intelligent, and less sensitive than she. She was picking men she could now "dominate." Her fear was of getting involved in a relationship with anyone "better," someone with whom there might be a chance of repeating the dynamics of her bad marriage — a relationship with a "strong" man.

The women on this weekend were a varied lot, aged twenty-three to fifty-three, most of them strangers to one another. There were any number of reasons to suppose we might not get along — age differences, some background differences, different personalities and temperaments. But what happened to us drew us together in ways none of us could have anticipated. In discovering our commonality, we discovered much to help us individually. We took away some real strength and hope to help us in the rest of our lives. Here's how that happened.

The main tasks of our weekend were to be physical. I know I was apprehensive about them, and many other women were too. We'd be biking, kayaking — stretching ourselves physically in ways most of us had never attempted before. But before we began, we were given a very special gift — the gift of watching, and then discussing among ourselves, a truly magical film.

Nobody's Child is the true story of a woman wrongly diagnosed as mentally ill and institutionalized for most of her life, and if you saw it on television when it first ran, you probably understand the critical acclaim it received. Marlo Thomas, who played the institutionalized woman, was superb. She captured this woman's plight so sensitively, and with such resonance, that there wasn't a woman in the room watching it who wasn't profoundly moved — and who didn't identify in some surprising ways.

The child in the title was a little girl, abandoned by her biological parents and adopted by a family with a cold and rejecting mother. Feeling angry and hurt and alone, the little girl threw tantrums, eventually having a "nervous breakdown" that landed her in the first of many institutions. She grew up being told that she was mentally ill, and she deteriorated to the point where it was decided she would probably have to be permanently institutionalized. She was so heavily medicated during one period that she neither walked nor talked for two years. The turning point of the story was one therapist's belief that there was a spark of life in this woman, and that she could be brought out of her anguished isolation. That therapist's belief paid off in amazing and heart-wrenching ways. With careful nurturing, the supposedly mentally ill woman began to speak, to walk, to come out of her shell. With love and support, she got to the point where she could learn skills and work . . . finally go to school . . . even marry. The woman's blossoming culmi-nated in her coming back to the institution in which she'd been confined for so many years, diagnosed as a hopeless case, to give a lecture to the staff as a guest speaker. Her triumph touched all of us. There wasn't a dry eye in the house.

Why were we so touched? The discussion we had after the film was a revelation. It wasn't simply that we felt sorry for the woman; we *identified* with her. We were all professional women, in varying degrees of successful com-mand of our lives, so why did we identify so strongly with someone like Nobody's Child — a woman who had faced a degree of abandonment and terror none of us had really known?

It turned out that our deepest fears were precisely the fears that the film had explored. Secretly, however secure our lives may have looked on the outside, we were fight-ing some powerful battles against insecurity. The fears we identified in ourselves ran the gamut: fear of extreme isolation and abandonment, of having to be on our own and not being able to make it, of somehow landing in the hands of someone who would mistreat or exploit us, of being out of control — "going off the deep end" — of being raped, of becoming a bag lady.

What was especially astonishing — and, in a sense,

wonderful — was how quickly these fears tumbled out of us, and how relieved we felt to admit them. It was clear to all of us that we were secretly fighting some forbidding dragons, and until now we hadn't shared with other women that we had held these terrors at bay for so long. One woman said, "It's like I live my life with one hand pushing a door shut, pushing with all my strength, a door that holds back the worst kind of calamity — and while I'm struggling to hold that door shut, I'm trying to live my life as if nothing were the matter. I never realized until now how hard the struggle in me was — the struggle of pretending that I'm secure and okay and everything's fine."

It was clear that whatever our individual tasks were — whatever specific issues we'd brought to this weekend to work on — we had in common a pool of fear, and, having watched this film, we already had moved closer to each other; we had already felt each other's support simply by sharing our fears with each other.

Now, however, came the work of beginning to get over them.

■ ■ ■ ■ ■ ■ ■ ■ ■ ■ ■ ■ ■ ■

Three-Point Emotional Fitness Program: How to Jump Hurdles You Never Thought You Could

In each of the following three points, I'll bring you through what the women on our "fear weekend" went through and learned, and then suggest ways that you can apply the same principles to challenge yourself. This is a chapter about emotional, not physical, fitness, and you certainly don't have to take twenty-mile bike rides or throw yourself down a river in a kayak to learn what we did. But to become the woman you want to be and to have the life you dream of having, you do have to challenge yourself to grow in emotional strength. Discovering ways to challenge yourself will be the task in this program.

1. Being with Yourself

The first physical task we set for ourselves was a very long bike ride — over twenty miles for those who could do it, as many miles toward that goal as the rest of us could accomplish. What we each promised ourselves was that we'd hang on for as long as we could, past the point where it was comfortable to keep going.

The most revealing lesson of our bike ride wasn't simply the state of our thigh muscles — although we did learn a lot about our physical endurance and strength. The bike ride was equally a test of our ability to be with ourselves. Few of us are used to listening to what comes up in our minds for any length of time. We continually block out our mind's messages with distractions. We hurriedly move from task to task, shopping, cleaning, reading, working, driving — whatever we can do to distract ourselves from the terrifying prospect of simply listening to our own minds. Each of us on the bike ride, however long we were able to last, had to face this terrifying prospect, with some interesting results. Many of us had never known what we were like in this way. Some women were amazed at the tapes they automatically played in their minds, either at how reflexively negative they were ("You'll never make it to the end of this, you're in lousy shape, all the other women are better than you") or, more positively, how creative the time they spent with themselves could be. Sharing what went on in our minds later was the real product of this bike hike. Those of us who'd berated ourselves learned that we could change the tape and be more positive, more creative in our thoughts; those who were already positive were overjoyed at what a creative resource they had in their minds. We learned that we had a lot to say to ourselves, and that we were better for having given ourselves time to listen to it.

The technique of giving yourself time to listen to yourself is crucial to becoming emotionally fit. We discovered in the last chapter how the Four Rs can give constructive form to our own mental analysis, but emotionally, it also helps to let your mind go free, with no constraints, allowing whatever comes up to come up and pass through. I find the best time to do this is during some kind of physical exercise, something repetitive, like walking on a treadmill — a mindless, solitary activity that allows my mind to free-fall.

You may be so used to distracting yourself that you don't realize that even music can shut you off from your thoughts. In your buried fear of meeting yourself, you may reach for a Walkman — music to take the place of thought, noise to block out what you might have to tell yourself. But don't. Pick a solitary exercise: walking is fine; or jogging, if you're at a level of fitness to do it safely and mindlessly; or swimming; or, as I do, walking on the treadmill at a gym. Then let your mind go in silence — let it take you anywhere and everywhere. I have some of my most creative thoughts at these moments. You can unleash your own creativity in the same way.

Not that you might not give yourself some resistance at first. A problem for most of us is that because we're not used to spending time with ourselves, when we start to do so we often automatically get negative. Sometimes the negative tapes are simple messages of impatience: "What am I doing this for? I don't have time to spend like this — I have so many things to do! How am I supposed to be creative? This is a waste of time."

Be ready for these negative tapes: we all play them. Be ready for them by having some positive replacements on hand — replacements you've taken the time to come up

with *before* you start your exercise. Look back again at
the negative maxims you identified for yourself back in
chapter 1, when you wrote your biography, and in chapter
2, when you considered Fact 8, "Life is on a rheostat."
Before you begin to walk, jog, swim, or get on the treadmill, spend some time looking at this list and replacing
each negative maxim with a positive counterpart — on
paper, so you'll have the list when you need it in the
future. Examples: "I'm lazy" can be turned into "I have
abundant energy when I love what I'm doing"; "I'll never
succeed," into "I have everything it takes to succeed"; or
"This is a waste of time," into "I'm thrilled to be taking
time for myself." Chant these affirmations while you exercise as if they were mantras: they'll start you on a positive, creative, and productive track.

It's important to keep at this for a minimum of thirty
minutes — even longer, if you can. Five-minute breaks
won't get the flow going, you need to give yourself time.
(A dividend is that spending at least thirty minutes at the
physical exercise will give you real aerobic benefits, too.)
You'll be amazed at the emotional fitness — and physical
fitness! — that soon results. You'll not only feel more
creative, but you'll experience a kind of buoyancy that
will carry over into the rest of your day.

2. Learning to "Think Aikido"

An extraordinary experience we had on our weekend was
discovering aikido, a martial art whose aim is to use the
aggressor's energy against the aggressor, to let hostile energy pass by and to use that energy so that it actually
works to your advantage. A good example of the principle
behind aikido is the movement of a skilled bullfighter:
confronted with a charging bull, he deftly moves aside so
that the beast affects him with no more than a passing
breeze. We weren't there to learn the physical side of
aikido but rather to appreciate the emotional side. The

lessons we learned were to have a stunning impact on all of us.

Women are especially conditioned and sensitized to overreact emotionally. Because of the message, deeply planted in us, that we're not in control of our lives — that somebody else is supposed to call the shots — when we sense that somebody else is attempting to control us, we often become either wildly defensive or grovelingly guilty. Issues of conflict escalate as a result: we often end up making things much worse than they have to be.

The aikido principle can help get us out of that tendency to overreact. We can learn to acknowledge someone's anger without giving in to it. We can listen to what they have to say, appraise what we hear, decide for ourselves whether or not it's accurate, and then decide how to address it. One woman in the group, Eileen, realized she already had begun to practice the aikido principle of flowing with hostile energy. She told us that she had gone through the embarrassment of having a large check bounce at a department store — evidently the funds she'd deposited to cover the check had just missed registering when the check came through her bank. "I was mortified," she said. "I'm meticulous about paying bills, and this is a real sore point with me; it pushes all my buttons when anyone accuses me of not paying bills on time." Matters weren't helped by the fact that the man at the department store who called to complain was angry and abusive. "It was like he thought I did this all the time," said Eileen. "But I took a deep breath," she continued, "and reminded myself I had a choice. I could blow up at the man with a lot of 'How dare you!'s or I could go with the flow and apologize. It was, after all, my responsibility: whatever the reasons the bank hadn't registered my deposit, as far as the department store was concerned, I was the one who was at fault."

Eileen said she was glad the man called, she didn't

know why it happened, but she knew it was her responsibility. When the man said the bounced check had cost
the company extra money, she quickly promised to pay
the penalty. She apologized — she simply accepted the
fact that it was her responsibility and her error. "The guy's
reaction was wonderful," she said. "It was like I took all
the wind out of his sails. He was expecting me to be
defensive, and here I was agreeing with him. We ended
the conversation amicably with him saying that he understood and that he was sure it wouldn't happen again."
She realized she'd come through this on the aikido principle — a principle, now that she had a name for it, she
was conscious she wanted to use again.

Thinking aikido means practicing acknowledging
someone else's point of view. It also means exercising the
muscle of restraint — a phrase I introduced in the last
chapter. When you allow a sudden storm of anger or de-
fensiveness to take over, your thinking is clouded and
your ability to respond in a thought-out manner is im-
paired. Waiting for the storm cloud to pass and then attempting to empathize with (so that you can understand)
the "hostile force" allows you to deal much more pro-
ductively with conflict — no matter how distressing. You
can defend yourself far more effectively if you don't act
defensive.

None of this is to suggest that you should apologize for
something you're not guilty of; rather, admitting whatever complicity you may have in the conflict will help
you to clarify the conflict. The aikido principle allows
you to see what the real forces in your life are — to see
and accept them for what they are so that you have a
realistic chance of dealing with them. Accepting circumstances in your life doesn't mean you shouldn't try to
change them; it allows you to see what those circumstances really *are* so that you can change them effectively.

The aikido principle of acceptance can be practiced in nearly everything you do, from dealing with a sullen checkout person at a supermarket to dealing with a re-calcitrant husband or angry boss. One woman I explained this principle to told me she'd found herself using it pro-ductively the very next day. She was in a department store and asked a salesperson how much a certain item was. The salesperson snapped back, "How should I know? This isn't my department." "My first impulse was to snap right back," my friend said, "but then I remembered what you said about aikido, and that I could accept even this surly woman for who she was. I even allowed myself an instant to identify with her — the store was frantically busy, and she did seem frazzled. So instead of getting angry and storming out of the store, which is what I might have done before, I asked her who I *could* speak to about the item I wanted to buy. She directed me to another person standing nearby, and she was even polite about it!"

3. Breaking Through Barriers: The "Just Do It" Principle

Probably the most frightening task the women on our weekend faced was kayaking — at least it was for me. I guess I wasn't totally unprepared for the kind of fear I felt about it: when I took up skiing three years ago, I was aware I was pushing myself to break through a major fear barrier in some of the same ways. The phobia I had about flying is related: the idea of going up in a ski lift and then plummeting down a mountain on skis seemed like the height of lunacy and something I wouldn't have at-tempted in a million years — until I realized that I was up against another debilitating fear, one that I knew I could benefit from facing. I'll never forget my first time on a ski lift: I closed my eyes and clung to my ski in-structor for dear life, not daring to look down. Even on "baby" hills I was petrified. At first I could only move laterally, across the hill instead of down it. Then my ski instructor said it was time to learn how to get to the bottom of the hill in a more direct fashion. I looked at him helplessly: I was terrified! But he encouraged me, and he taught me something valuable in doing so. He stuck in a ski pole a dozen feet ahead of me and told me to ski only to that point. I could manage that — and I did. Then, in equally short clips, I found myself going down the hill. I wasn't close to speeding down the way others were, but I was doing it! I'd broken through another barrier. And the exhilaration was amazing. I told everyone I knew that I'd managed to ski straight down my "baby" hill. It didn't matter if nobody else was impressed — I knew what a feat I'd accomplished!

Kayaking provoked similar fears — in some ways, worse ones. If you've ever gotten into a kayak you know that it's almost more accurate to say you put it on than you get into it. The interior of the boat is molded to your legs, and the skirt that you wear around your waist, which is attached to the kayak, seals you in as if you were a bottle top. It's not easy getting out of a kayak once you're in one.

Going down a river in a kayak often means going down *into* the river; it's easy to turn over and find you're traveling with your head underwater. Much of our instruction had to do with getting out of the kayak if we capsized. I know I wasn't the only woman who suffered from fear here, everything from the claustrophobia of having your lower body trapped in the kayak to the terror of drowning. What a triumph it was when each of us discovered how to maneuver: how to get out of the kayak when it went over, how to make it do what *we* wanted it to do. It was breaking through a barrier of fear few of us thought we could manage when we started out. (One woman confessed that she went away for a few minutes on her own to "have a little cry" before coming back to get into her kayak. All of us sympathized.)

Susan Jeffers wrote a book whose title sums up the main lesson we learned from our kayaking adventure: *Feel the Fear and Do It Anyhow*. I can't tell you how liberating it is to break through the barrier of fear, to prove to yourself that you can come out intact on the other side. As I said at the beginning of this chapter, you don't have to do anything as physically forbidding as kayaking or taking endless bike hikes; in fact, determining what fear to break through is a very personal matter — one between you and you. But we can turn this principle into emotional fitness exercises simply by suggesting that you do two things, one big, the other small. First the big one:

■■■■■■■■■■■■■■

Plan a Challenging Experience Once a Year

Depending on interests, finances, and time, your challenging experience can range from a solo trip to Kathmandu to taking yourself out to a restaurant alone for the first time. Attach the fear you want to conquer to something you've always wanted to do but never dared imagine you could accomplish. This might involve travel, if not quite to Kathmandu then perhaps to a neighboring city you've always wanted to visit on your own. It might involve taking a public-speaking course; that's a big fear for many people, and learning to address a group is one of the most wonderful ways of building self-confidence. It might involve giving a party for more people than you've ever invited — a really large buffet, with an interesting, even daring, mix of people, people you may always have wanted to meet but haven't had the courage to speak to, much less invite to a party. Look at the hierarchy of your fears and choose one of the really big ones — but one attached to something you know will give you pleasure when you accomplish it.

The benefits from this aren't limited to the fearful event itself: you'll give yourself the pleasure (or at least the instructive experience) of anticipating it and remembering it as well as actually going through it. Make it a big deal. You're facing something you're afraid of, and you can't congratulate yourself enough for doing that.

The other version of this exercise is simply:

■■■■■■■■■■■■■■■

Break Your Fear Barrier Every Twenty-four Hours — Even in a Small Way

You always have an opportunity to do this. Whether it's dealing with an irate creditor, as the woman with the bounced check had to do; making a difficult phone call; completing a particularly onerous task that you know has to be done but you'd love to put off; asking for a raise you know you deserve; deciding to go to a movie or an art gallery alone — there are any number of daily opportunities to face your fears. Make your motto simple: Just Do It. I promise that it won't feel like self-punishment. Instead you will feel the immense satisfaction that comes from facing your fears, a satisfaction that grows and bolsters your self-esteem the more frequently you earn it. Emotional fitness is the dividend. That buoyancy I spoke of earlier will become more reliable. You'll find that you are developing the resources to meet anything life hands out the more you practice the Just Do It principle. Sure, you may have to sweat. Sure, you may not love it. Sure, it means going through some pain. But remember what we said about the parallels to physical exercise? Fitness comes through challenge. You're not doing this to punish yourself. You're doing it to have a better life.

■■■■■■■■■■■■■■■

Finally, Reward Yourself

For every major fear I pass through, I buy myself a marker gift, something related to the feat I've accomplished, something to remind me what I've done and help me to feel good about myself. One nice way of doing this is to begin a charm bracelet: buy a new charm every time you've jumped a fear hurdle and have it relate to whatever the hurdle was. If you took yourself to Paris, get a charm of the Eiffel Tower. If you faced up to your boss after years of cringing and kowtowing, get a charm that reminds you of that victory — a laurel wreath, perhaps. If you made yourself give a big party, buy yourself a charm in the shape of a champagne bottle or a wrapped package. Use your imagination: make these reminders personal, something only you will understand. You'll find that when you look at each of those charms you'll be able to remind yourself not only of the particular triumphs they represent, but of a more general triumph in your life: you've proven again and again that you can face up to your fears. You've now got the medals to prove it. Let that charm bracelet be your soldier's medals. You've won them in some difficult battles, haven't you?

Reward yourself with people, too. As much as facing fear is a solitary act, one of the greatest gifts of my weekend in Colorado was the realization of how close women can become if they'll only share what they really feel with one another. Share your fears and your triumphs with friends you know you can trust — and invite them to share their fears and triumphs with you. And if you can find a video copy of *Nobody's Child* — to help you face the most secret and terrifying of your fears and share them with a group of women the way I did — I can't imagine a better way of getting things rolling. No matter how strange or unique or foolish you may think your own fears are, I guarantee that other women share them. Talking about those fears with others can be wonderfully healing. But practicing our emotional fitness exercises will actually help you to *do* something about them. And that's what emotional fitness is really all about.

5

··············

Decisions, Decisions . . .

··················

IF you've carried out the exercises I've given you so far, you've already begun to experiment with making changes in your life. A dividend is almost certainly that your attitude about being *able* to change is more positive: you now realize you do have power over certain aspects of your life because you've already begun to exercise it. You *can* rely on yourself for direction after all. As you grow in self-confidence and resilience, which you will with the help of the emotional fitness pointers we've just explored, you'll simply bolster this positive attitude, make it even more positive. The apparatus of your life is already in better working order than it was even a short while ago.

Learning to make your own decisions is the real lesson of all this. Decisions give your life direction. And without direction, you're obviously — quite literally — nowhere.

If you don't know where you're going, any road will take you there. And what's worse, if your life lacks direction, you may already be as far as you'll ever get right now. It may have been the despair of thinking you were at a dead end that brought you to this book. You may have already realized a simple truth: a life without direction is like a car without a driver — full of potential, but useless until somebody turns on the ignition, puts a foot on the gas pedal, and steers it onto the road.

Women so often jump out of their lives as if their lives were cars, relinquishing the keys to someone else as if to say, "Here — you drive." Even the simplest decisions can sometimes stop us in our tracks: "What should I do?" is a question usually directed to someone outside yourself, which means the answers you get about your life come from others. We're already seen this as a major problem, and you've already begun to deal with it by following some specific directions about charting your own path. But because decision making is so important and such an ongoing part of life, we need to pay even closer attention to the process. Every decision you make is an opportunity — and a doorway to change. Let's look a little harder at how we approach and open those doors.

It's no secret that life is composed of big and little decisions. Or that, for some of these decisions, outside help is imperative. If you face a medical emergency, it's foolish not to see a doctor. If you need to learn a new skill, it's foolish not to seek instruction from an expert. There are, however, many more decisions about which the best expert is you — decisions not only about what color to paint the bedroom, what dress to wear on Saturday night, but about career and men and family. Making these decisions as consciously as possible has far-reaching ramifications: you will find yourself on a particular road of your own choosing and you'll have the satisfaction of knowing *you* chose it. That satisfaction is one of the most wonderful things you can experience: the feeling that you deserve the credit for what you've done in your life because you've accepted responsibility for your decisions.

Maybe this scares you. The very word *responsibility* can seem intimidating: if you choose, doesn't that mean if it goes wrong it's your fault?

Taking responsibility for your life — which means for the decisions you make in your life — doesn't have to be terrifying. We've already seen that rejection won't kill you and that you can learn from your mistakes, and we'll see more vivid examples of what it's like to learn from what appear to be missteps as we go on. But what none of this prepares you for is the feeling of freedom responsibility can give you. Once you truly acknowledge your own part in your decisions and your relationships, you give yourself power, you don't take power away. You see that everything in your life is affected by choice — your choice — which also suggests that you've got the power to make new choices: you can choose to alter whatever you feel needs altering. When you live your life with your whole self, which you will when you take responsibility for it, you're no longer dependent on what other people think. You may care about what they think, but you won't be dependent on their approval.

However, before you can get to the point where you truly feel you've taken over the reins of your life, you may have to do some housecleaning. You may feel like jumping on a horse and charging into battle, but if you find yourself worrying about what horse to choose, what to wear on the ride, what saddle is best — if you clench at the preliminary and less important decisions so that you can't ever get going — you need some help with perspective.

Sorting out priorities isn't always easy. The only way to get rid of the unnecessary mental clutter that may crowd into your mind, confuse you, and impair your decision-making ability is to call a halt, calm down, and ask yourself a simple question: "What do I really want?" Answering this question can take courage — the courage to be honest, to face the *whole* truth about yourself.

■■■■■■■■■■■■■■

Getting Honest with Yourself

Making good decisions requires self-honesty. You may think you've got an open mind, but unconsciously you may have already decided what the answer has to be. And because you're divided against yourself — outwardly deciding one thing but inwardly deciding another — it's no surprise if you're miserable.

Sandra illustrates this dilemma very well. She's an attractive, thirty-eight-year-old woman who realizes at least superficially that she has a lot of potential, but she cannot ever seem to land that perfect situation — that dream job that will make everything right. Sandra is an actress who is fed up with making the rounds. "Hollywood's the pits," she says. "How can you get a job when they're hiring twenty-three-year-olds to play middle-aged women?" Sandra decided she had to give up "calling myself an actress" and get a "real job." So she diligently searched the newspaper classified ads, called friends, and took courses in typing and word processing. Sandra proudly told everyone around her that she was perfectly willing to enter the "real world," and she wasn't too proud to start with something on an entry level either.

But Sandra doesn't like getting up early in the morning. She likes her afternoon naps. The years she's spent making the rounds as an actress, getting the occasional job but never working for too long at a stretch, have conditioned her to a certain way of life. And so, somehow, no job she's been offered has ever had quite the benefits she is seeking — the salary wasn't good enough, there was no dental plan, it wasn't in the part of town she wanted to work in — and Sandra remains jobless, hoping she can survive on what little income her parents are contributing.

There's nothing wrong with not wanting to get up early or taking the occasional afternoon nap. But for Sandra to make a positive move in her life, she has to wake up to her real agenda: she has to admit to herself that she's wasting her time interviewing for jobs that would require her to work nine to five. She might then consider part-time work or evening work or work she could do at home — there are any number of options that could be open to her. She might also consider changing the way she views nine-to-five work — maybe challenge herself by trying something different to see what happens. But she has access to none of these options until she wakes up to some unconscious decisions she's already made about what she's willing to do and what she isn't.

Are you holding yourself back without knowing it — or admitting it? Sometimes asking yourself questions about patterns that seem to recur — the "same old thing" stopping you in your tracks — can reveal some inner decisions you've made that you have not been willing to see. Perhaps, like Sandra, you just don't want to admit that you like afternoon naps. Maybe you feel guilty about the fact that you don't like to get up early, or that certain things matter to you that may seem frivolous or unimportant to somebody else.

However, you'll remain stuck if you don't take a hard look at what's really motivating you, and what you are willing to do to get what you want. Pretending you're somebody you aren't isn't doing anyone any good, least of all yourself. If you are stuck, if, despite all efforts to move forward, you continue to spin your wheels, ask yourself the following self-diagnostic questions. Write them down in the journal into which you've put the rest of your answers to questions in this book: the data you're amassing about yourself won't be helpful only today, it will also help in the future to look back at the truth you were able to tell yourself. You're giving your future self courage and direction by being honest with yourself now.

1. Have I felt this kind of confusion about my life before? If so, when?

2. Are there similarities between then and now? What are they?

3. If I could have anything I wanted in the world — no matter what it was or how silly it might sound to anyone else — what would it be?

4. Am I trying to make myself do something totally the opposite of what I really want?

5. Is what I want important enough to motivate me to change aspects of my behavior and life-style?

6. Can I break down my ultimate goal into smaller, manageable tasks I can accomplish more easily?

7. Do I have the patience and resolve to accomplish these smaller tasks in service of my ultimate goal?

8. When I've determined my ultimate goal, am I willing to pay the price — sacrifice time or money or certain benefits I now have so that I can attain this goal?

Your answers to these questions will enable you to see if what you're thinking about doing is something you're really willing to do. You need to ask yourself about not only your desire but your willingness to sacrifice to attain that desire. The balance you're seeking is between pipe dream and cynicism. Deciding wisely means charting a course that teaches you that it's wonderful to dream and even more wonderful to work to achieve that dream. Your answers to these questions will tell you whether or not you truly want to chart that course.

■■■■■■■■■■■■■■■

Owning Your Course

Once you've decided that this *is* the course you want to take, the secret of staying on that course is to remind yourself continually that it is *your decision* to follow it. In other words, "own" whatever course you choose — take responsibility for it, see it as something you are doing for yourself. When you make your life your personal mission, when you see it as the product of changes you yourself initiate, you take care of it. Imagine that your goal is your child: give it all the love and care you'd give your own child, make sure you're doing everything you can to bring it up well. If you do this, you won't be buffeted by other people's opinions or disapproval because you won't care so much about them. Neither will you complain or blame anyone else when things go wrong. Your goal *is* the child of your dreams, which means it's your complete responsibility. It has nothing to do with anything or anybody else.

A dramatic example of learning to take charge of your own life is Beverly, a woman who has taught herself to be sensitive to her real needs and bases her decisions on what she continually finds out about herself. Beverly worked for fifteen years as an international producer: it was a terribly demanding job, and she grew more and more unhappy as the stress got worse from year to year. Finally she decided she needed to take some time off. It was during what she had first planned to be only a vacation that she discovered a lump in her breast: she was diagnosed with breast cancer. "This felt like the last straw," Beverly says. "I'd finally decided to ease up the pressure on myself, and suddenly my body betrays me. It was an awful time." Beverly opted for a lumpectomy, which she was told would probably get rid of the cancer for good, although the next five years would be the test. Beverly made a decision.

"My life felt like it was on the line, for the first time ever. I didn't want to go back to my career — I finally allowed myself to realize I'd come to hate it. Suppose I only had a year left to live, or two? Things fell into an entirely different perspective. My priorities shifted." Beverly made the decision to leave her job and move to an entirely new area — California. She had asked herself the third question on our list — "If I could have anything I wanted in the world, what would it be?" — and realized she'd always wanted to live in a warm climate. Ever since she was a little girl, she'd dreamed of California: "I wanted to be in the sun, and I dreamed of being able to see the Pacific from my window." So she uprooted herself from New York and made the move. "I knew my family wouldn't be pleased about my moving so far away, but I also knew I didn't get the support from them I needed. I didn't want to be embroiled in their seemingly endless squabbles and problems, not while I was healing." Beverly's mother, especially, tended to be a worrier and a meddler, and Beverly knew her sanity and physical health depended on keeping a safe distance. "I felt bad telling my mother I wanted to move to the other coast, but I knew it was the right decision for me, even if my family couldn't understand." Beverly had enough savings to rent a small house near the ocean in Southern California and live frugally. Slowly, she awakened to new desires and had new insights about herself. She became a vegetarian. She went to a nutritionist. Later, she learned how to meditate. A year or so after that, she took acting classes at UCLA and started going to Jane Fonda's gym. She made new friends and enjoyed a quiet and slow pace, so different from the hectic life she'd once led as a producer. The five-year danger mark approached — and passed. Her doctor gave her a clean bill of health. Beverly knew she had put herself into a healing environment, that she had done all she could to maintain and improve her health. Refreshed, she was now ready to consider going back to work. She wanted to explore relationships on a deeper level, too, perhaps even marry. Money was getting tight — she'd been living on savings all this time — and she had to get some help from friends. She was delighted to see that she'd made friends who really cared about her and were willing to give generously while she got herself back into the work world. Beverly got a few freelance consulting jobs, then was offered permanent work. Her fears returned: the job was in New York, back in the rat race she'd fled five years before. But her new, stronger self had emerged, and she began to see the job as an opportunity — a challenge instead of a crisis. Gone was the fear of going back to New York as a needy, ready-to-do-anything-to-avoid-conflict child. Gone was the girl out to prove she was as good as any man. Gone was the female who was once unsure she was a grown-up woman.

"It was like I had taught myself to grow up," Beverly says. "It's taken me forty years to get to a point where I can really call myself an adult woman. That doesn't mean having an 'impressive' job or an 'impressive' husband or family. What it means is that I've learned who I am — what my loves and hates are — and I've developed the courage to direct my own life so that I have the greatest chance of getting what I want. I guess you could say I've finally heard — and heeded — my own voice."

Beverly went through some necessary rites of passage

before she could reclaim her life and feel fully confident that she is capable of following her own voice. The goals that are now clear to her are clear because she's discovered them in herself. As she puts it, "It's wonderful to look in the mirror and know exactly who the person is looking back at you." She was honest enough with herself at that turning point five years ago to call a halt to situations she knew were damaging. "It wasn't only my job making me crazy; my family was getting too much for me, too. It was a personal affront to my mother if a day went by without my calling her," Beverly says. "All of it was endangering my health — which meant I had to detach from it." Having learned to do that, she now has clear boundaries in her life, which others have come to respect ("Although," Beverly says, "it took my mother some time to get used to it."). She knows now what she is willing to give — and what she feels the right to *ask* of others.

These boundaries are hard won. Women so often allow themselves to be trampled on because they feel that they're supposed to be endlessly giving, endlessly available. We can now see that that kind of endless receptivity is a result of conditioning — conditioning that taught you to hand over your power to somebody else. It takes great strength to recognize what you are willing to give to, and accept from, other people. You have to pay attention to your own desires, needs, and wants and weigh them against what others want from you. Beverly is thrilled to have learned this.

But what Beverly is especially thrilled to have learned is that she's grown up. Growing up means, she now knows, achieving certain specific goals. In fact, I've identified seven goals that, once achieved, signal adulthood. They mark certain rites of passage, the fulfillment of which separates girls, who avoid change at all costs, from women, who know that having a satisfying life requires responsibility and flexibility and, above all, the willing-ness to change. When your decisions serve the following goals — when, in one way or another, your decisions help you to move closer to achieving these goals — you're doing all you can to move toward lasting fulfillment.

■■■■■■■■■■■■■■

Decide Your Way to Adulthood: Seven Goals for the Grown-up Woman

1. To have marketable skills in order to be economically self-supporting.

This may seem obvious, but you cannot truly make choices or depend on yourself if you are not capable of supporting yourself. At every age and stage of life, a woman needs to be her own insurance policy, even if she's currently married and handsomely supported by her hus-band: that support could disappear very quickly, for any number of reasons. Having a marketable skill is one of the most important goals a woman can set for herself. If you've never supported yourself before, take steps to de-velop that marketable skill now. Try to capitalize on your interests — for example, take a part-time job in a depart-ment store to determine how interested you really are in a retail-sales career; volunteer at a hospital to see if you really do want to work with sick people; become a teach-er's aide to see if you want to deal with children for a living. But gear even volunteer work to a career: find out how to get *paid* for work you want to do. It's always a good idea to talk to women who are doing what they want to do — what roads did they travel to get where they are today?

The simple truth is that you need to take steps to en-sure that you have the ability to be self-supporting no matter what your current marital or financial status is. True self-reliance can't happen if you're not able to pay your own way. Money may not be able to buy happiness, but it can certainly help to buy freedom: the ability to earn money means the ability to say no. It's an ability that does more than give you financial freedom — it's also a very effective means of gaining self-respect.

2. To be fulfilled and happy on your own, even if you choose to be with a mate.

This is a hard one for many women. But it's a crucial goal. The statistical reality is that we will live a significant part of our lives alone, due to death or divorce or desertion. As I've already said, you can't *expect* to live all your life with a man. We have to learn to enjoy our own company; that's why my emphasis has so often been on learning to do things solo. It means learning that you're sufficient with or without male company. This doesn't mean isolating yourself from other people. Friends are some of the most important assets anyone can have. Even if there's no special man in your life, that doesn't mean you don't have access to people, men *and* women. And don't be put off if others give knowing winks when you say you and a man are just friends. While friendship between a man and a woman may mean many things over the course of a relationship, some of the best friends you can have are men. The point is, whatever your relationship status, it's important to feel good about who you are, so you can enjoy your own company. The relationship you have with yourself is the only relationship you know you will have for a lifetime.

How can you learn to like being with yourself? Give yourself something you enjoy doing. Go to an art gallery, join an English literature class, or take a ceramics course. Explore music: volunteer for a chorus or get a concert subscription. Begin a collection you know will interest you and take antiquing trips to add to it. Develop a life-long sport like swimming, golf, or hiking. There are any number of ways to enjoy your own company, as long as you let your interests guide you.

There's another dividend in learning to enjoy being you: others pick up on it. Think of the people you like and are drawn to: isn't it evident that they like them-selves? Don't they radiate comfort with being who they are? Now think of the people you tend to avoid. Do they communicate extreme neediness, discomfort with them-selves? The fact is, you'll draw others to you if you enjoy being you. And you won't if you don't.

> *3. To acknowledge that you are the major contributor to your own life — that you have consented to be who and where you are by the things you've said yes and no to.*

I can hear some distant thunder, the "But-what-abouts" that you may be piling up in response to this goal. "But what about my husband? He's the one whose income I depend on, he's the one who bought the house we live in. . . ." "But what about the fact that I never had any advantages — never received money to go to college, never received the love I deserved, never . . . never . . . never . . . ?" You already know the answer to "but" or "if only." The fact is that wherever you are right now, you're still there because at some point, in one fashion or an-other, you consented to be there. This isn't to blame you for your plight, if you're in one. It's merely to help you recognize your contribution to the life you have right now, whether it was by design (conscious choice) or de-fault (allowing someone else to decide). I don't mean that you may not have had to deal with real hardships and that many of the decisions you've made have been in response to them. Perhaps you're a single mother whose ex-husband is supposed to pay child support but doesn't, and the courts can't move fast enough to do anything about next month's rent. Perhaps you're a woman of fifty-eight who's never worked outside the home, but now, with an ill and bed-ridden husband, you desperately need the extra income and haven't a clue where to turn. Perhaps you're a woman of twenty-one whose parents have thrown you out because you just got pregnant and you do not want to marry the father — and you'll have to fight for child support. Life can throw us some terrible surprises, and it would be wrong to suggest that it's all your fault or that there's a simple way out. Certainly there are times when circumstances work against us and we find ourselves in situations we could never have seen coming. But how we respond to what happens to us is our responsibility. After all, who else's could it be?

A crucial aspect of growing up is realizing that no one is waiting in the wings to come to our rescue every time we need someone. We have to be prepared to come to our own rescue, whether it's bailing ourselves out of financial trouble by seeking ways to make more money (rather than hoping desperately that someone else will pay our bills) or learning new skills, meeting new people, going new places — all in an attempt to get a better job and have a better life. When we need help, the best first thing is to see how much of that help we have the power to provide for ourselves. Sometimes helping ourselves means seeking appropriate aid or information from others. But the point is to make decisions that reflect the fact that we are willing to take care of ourselves. We need to remember the great degree of our own consent in any situation we're in: as adults, we have chosen the people we love; we chose to say yes to that job, no to the other; we chose to eat, drink, smoke, spend too much — or to go for help if we found we couldn't stop self-destructive behavior; we are the ones who've decided nearly everything about what we have in our lives.

When you accept the fact that you're the producer, director, scriptwriter, and star of your own life, you accept something important about decision making. You recognize that you — not fate or your mother or husband or boss — are responsible for your situation and whatever is good or not so good in that situation. As I've already suggested, this gives you an enormous sense of freedom, a true freedom of choice. Now, when you tell yourself you couldn't possibly do something, perhaps you'll take a moment to reconsider and ask yourself: "Who's stopping me?"

4. To seek people who respect and appreciate you, and to respect and appreciate the people you choose to be with.

This is an essential goal, and it's one too many women don't achieve. Often it's because a woman doesn't feel worthy of better relationships, romantic or otherwise, so she keeps herself trapped in abusive job or marital situations she doesn't feel she has the right to change. She may fear that if she gives up the man she's with she'll never find another. This kind of low self-esteem can't help holding you back. The fact is, when you feel you deserve respect and appreciation, you will seek people who can give it to you; similarly, you will seek people whom you can respect and admire.

However, as I've said, feeling respect for yourself and others, feeling appreciated and appreciating others is far from what many women allow themselves. Out of fear, women often confuse love and need, which means they never learn what real love is all about. They will trade their bodies and self-respect for the ability to say they have a man in their lives. Sooner or later, they find out that's not enough, that they've sold themselves woefully short. I know that the reasons you may not feel you deserve more than this may have deep roots, but you deserve, right now, to realize that you're entitled to more from a man than his mere presence. You deserve to realize, right now, that you don't have to let your family or boss or children take advantage of you. But sometimes you have to wake up to the ways you may unwittingly *invite* exploitation.

Sixty-three-year-old Kate described herself as everyone's grandmother. The bookkeeper at a small business, it was Kate who made the coffee, Kate who always had the aspirin or vitamins or cough medicine when you needed them, Kate who always brought in home-baked coffee cake, Kate you could always count on to change the postal meter, take the mail to the post office. "I never had children," she said, "and my husband died about five years ago. I guess I never thought I was, well, *worthy*, if I didn't pay my way by taking care of people." All her friends, she said, were becoming grandparents; they all seemed to have such full lives. "All I had was my office. I'd turned the twelve people I saw every day into my family." When anyone had a birthday, Kate was there with a cake, and it was Kate who organized the office to get a card and gift. Then, one day, it was Kate's birthday.

"No one knew," she said. "My husband had died just the year before, and he always helped me celebrate, but this year I had no one. I came into the office that morning to make coffee as usual, take care of the office things as I usually did. And my coworkers started filing in — and I noticed something. Not one of them really said hello to me. 'Coffee ready, Kate?' 'My pencils sharpened?' 'Is the date on the postal meter changed?' I felt this terrible sinking feeling of aloneness. I almost wanted to cry." Kate couldn't be angry with her coworkers; she began to realize that she'd set up her situation herself. "It hit me that no one knew it was my birthday because I hadn't told anyone. And that made me realize no one paid the same kind of attention to me that I paid to them because I hadn't allowed them to. I was the one who took care of everyone; no one thought of reciprocating."

Kate realized how inappropriate it had been for her to lavish all her care on the people she worked with. "It's not that suddenly I don't care about them; I just realize I can't turn them into my *family*. And that I can't pin how I feel about myself on them." She has started to spend more time with friends outside of work, to increase the circle of friends she *can* depend on. And she doesn't automatically jump to do everything at work. "People still like me, even if I don't do everything for them. And this is teaching me to like myself a little better. I feel I deserve more than to be taken for granted, the way I once was. And now I'm seeking out people who won't take me for granted. If I can do it, after being the doormat I was for so many years, anyone can."

Feeling worthy is the premise of a happy life: it is the prerequisite for achieving any kind of lasting satisfaction. Look at your environment and see what it says about your feeling of self-worth. Are you allowing yourself to be exploited? Do you receive praise of any kind from people around you? Do you like the people you spend time with? Are they people you admire, want to emulate?

You will quickly realize whether or not you've surrounded yourself with people who are nurturing and supportive. If you haven't, the answer isn't suddenly to drop everyone in your life and replace them with others. The answer is to ask yourself why you allowed yourself to get involved with people who don't support you — why you felt you needed them. You need to begin a process of distancing so that, ultimately, you can let go of the negative dynamics to which you may now be attached. You may want to see a therapist to help you with this distancing process. But it is achievable. You can learn to respect and like yourself — and to seek out people who respect and like you. In fact, when you improve your own self-view, you'll find that you'll naturally gravitate to positive people, and they'll naturally be drawn to you.

5. To take all the measures you can to provide for people who depend on you.

If you accept the responsibility of having and bringing up children, you've made a pact with yourself to provide for them the best you can. This responsibility begins in pregnancy; undermining your own health while you're pregnant by eating badly, smoking, or drinking is a breach of the pact you've made to have a child. It is equally irresponsible to consider having a child if you don't have a realistic plan to give that child a home, food, and clothing. The point is, you don't take on responsibility for which you haven't prepared. Making the rash decision that you want a child, without having taken any measures to make sure you can bring that child up, is cruel to both of you.

People you have agreed to care for — and they might be sick or elderly parents and relatives as well as children — are special responsibilities. It's understandable, however, if you feel ambivalent about them. We've been given strongly contrasting cultural messages about nurturing, especially in the past twenty-five years. Dr. Paula Caplan's book *The Myth of Women's Masochism* argues that women have unfairly been told that their nurturing instincts made them somehow weaker, inferior — less than the stronger and allegedly more reliable and objective male. Some feminists have jumped on this particular bandwagon and made it seem, at times, like a sin for a

woman to be too caring, as if caring always meant neurotic acquiescence. This feminist backlash sometimes
gives the impression that it is wrong even to think of
taking care of anybody besides ourselves. But that kind
of "me first" attitude is selfish — and self-defeating. Remember Betty Friedan's call for balance that I mentioned
at the very beginning of this book? That balance means
taking our caring and nurturing talents and responsibilities seriously, giving them their full measure of worth.
It's true that it's limiting to define ourselves totally as
caretakers: our lives continue to belong to us even if, for
certain periods, we feel the need to devote them to someone else's well-being. But the truth is, we do have to take
care of people who depend on us.

Obviously this isn't limited to family members. You
have an equal responsibility to follow through on any job
you've agreed to do. Being a grown-up means accepting
that responsibility. Living a fulfilling life means enjoying
that responsibility as much as you can, accepting it *willingly.*

6. To be involved in "the family of man," to make the world a better place.

The poor spinning planet all of us inhabit is at our mercy.
Everything we do has an effect, not only on our own
individual lives, but on each other. Accepting this truth
means accepting a certain kind of responsibility. The philosophy I bring to this responsibility is what is called
altruistic egoism, which you may remember I defined in
chapter 2 as doing for yourself and others. Making a commitment to give to yourself and others in tandem. To
make the world better by your having existed. (Remember
how Jenny transformed her pain about her son's death
from leukemia into an inducement to work for leukemia
research?) By practicing altruistic egoism, I give myself

an important motivation, one that, when I follow it, brings me some of the most profound satisfaction I've experienced in my life.

I'm not suggesting that you have to renounce all worldly goods and become Mother Teresa, Gandhi, or Eleanor Roosevelt (not that they aren't perfectly good role models!) But the connection between ourselves and the world makes it painfully clear that we need to make an effort to contribute to it. Until we figure out a way to populate other planets, this world is all we have.

"But what can I do?" you ask. Certainly I'm not suggesting that you get on the next plane to Moscow and have a chat with Mr. Gorbachev about world peace. Opportunities for making a beneficial contribution to the world can start right where you are, right now. This productive work might mean joining a neighborhood watch to make sure the streets around your home are patrolled and safe. It might mean working one night a week in a soup kitchen, contributing to a fund to provide legal services to poor women, offering to feed a family at Thanksgiving, or contributing five dollars a week to a restaurant so that a homeless person can have a meal there. It also means doing the best you can at whatever job you do — being honest, having integrity, caring about your own efficiency and productivity. It may mean tackling some of the larger issues, too, by getting involved in organizations that fight pollution, toxic waste, violence.

Doing what I call productive work — work that touches other human beings, eases somebody else's path, improves a situation — serves you and others at the same time. It's service that connects you to other people and gives you a feeling of purpose. Productive work is healing work, and you can always find creative ways to do it. Anything you do that makes a positive difference in somebody else's life will make a positive difference in yours.

When you make a decision to do something that will leave your mark in this way on the lives of others, the rewards you receive will be long-lasting — and immeasurable.

> 7. *To make peace with your past, to forgive*
> *yourself for making mistakes without dwelling*
> *on them, and to go forward with your life.*

Most of us live our lives in the future when we're young ("I can't wait until I'm eighteen . . . get a car . . . leave home"), only to live our lives in the past as adults ("If only I had gone to college . . . hadn't gotten married so young . . . waited to have children . . . gone to law school"). Some of us never let go of our past mistakes, whether real or imagined ("Why did I have an abortion? How could I have left the hospital and my mother and not realized she was about to die? Why couldn't I see what a cheat my first husband was?"). We need to learn to let all of this go, to stop obsessing over a past we cannot change.

So many women look at the mistakes they've made as "wreckage" that blocks their current lives. But that wreckage doesn't have to block you; in fact, your past mistakes don't have to have any effect on the decisions you make now, except to provide lessons to be learned. Looking back healthily at your past can be likened to driving a car and glancing into the rearview mirror: you see if anything "dangerous" might be coming up and take appropriate measures to get out of its way, but you don't stare at the reflection in that rearview mirror; if you do, you can bank on driving off the road and suffering a crash. Look ahead of you: only glance back to gain perspective, to keep yourself "aligned." That's the way to deal with your past: look at it without morally judging yourself, see yourself as you were then and feel compassion for the "you that was," compare the old you with who you are now, and then return to what's ahead of you. You can learn from your past experiences without letting them drag you down.

Healthy decision making depends on a lot of factors. It is also what makes an adult an adult: we grow up when we take full responsibility for our own actions, when, as the saying goes, we "own" our lives. Few of us haven't been besieged by crises — things that we could never have anticipated, that we never dreamed would happen to us. As adults, we need to be vigilant. We need to monitor our lives, to realign ourselves continually so that we know we are not just reacting reflexively to life, but responding consciously to it. And if, inevitably, we make some mistakes — if the old reflexive, negative self rears its head and has its temporary way — we always have the choice to change direction. Realizing you *can* change direction is a lot of what being grown-up — and opening the door to lasting fulfillment — is all about.

6

....

With Him . . .

....

I SAID at the outset that this was not a book about men or about dealing with romantic problems with men. Our focus is so much more importantly on increasing your own sense of personal power over your life, discovering you have the confidence and the resources to start building the life you want — for *yourself*.

Up to now in this book, we have discussed men mainly in the context of realizing we don't have to rely on them for security, purpose, or direction. However, we'd all be lying if we pretended that men weren't still at or near the center of our most private dreams and perplexing dilemmas. I also said at the outset that women never sabotage themselves more than when they become romantically involved. Our definitions of happiness include love, and it is important that they do. This means we have to take a look from our new and growing sense of self-reliance at what we do to ourselves in the name of love. Can the principles we've been learning help us even in *this* mine-laden territory?

In a word, yes. You don't have to lose yourself when you enter the love realm, as you'll see from the evidence in this chapter. But first we must ask, why is it so difficult for most women to keep their heads around men?

Nowhere does our self-esteem seem more dependent on approval than when we reach out to a man with love. As independent as we may pride ourselves on being in every other aspect of our lives, the terrible inner fears and doubts most of us have been conditioned to feel about men — "Will he like me? Does he find me attractive? Does he think I'm a good lover? Does he like *her* better?" — still plague us. The profusion of books on how to find, keep, and deal with men bears clear witness to the fact that we haven't yet resolved these insecurities.

I'm not especially going to resolve them here, either, although I may give you some pointers that will help *you* to do so to a greater degree than you may have thought possible. What I want you to do is to take a look at this dilemma so that you can see, perhaps for the first time, some of the ways you trap yourself in love. This will enable you to call on inner resources to extricate yourself or to avoid getting trapped in the first place.

Because we live in a new, more liberated era doesn't mean that we aren't still besieged by some old messages that tell us men and women are unalterably separate species. In some ways, we find evidence that the gap between us is as wide as ever. In the movie *When Harry Met Sally* . . . Harry, a contemporary, up-to-the-minute, 1990s male, says something you might have expected from a vintage 1950s male chauvinist. Men, Harry states unequivocally, can't be friends with women.

Can we still be hearing this? Wasn't all that taken care of in the tumultuous decades we've just lived through? Didn't at least the more advanced of us finally get the message that men and women don't have to be at war with each other, that our relationships could be something other than sexual or combative? Or could Harry be right: is friendship impossible between the sexes because sex keeps getting in the way?

It's true that sex, among other things, can complicate friendship between men and women. But — sorry, Harry — men can become some of the best friends you will ever have and give you the greatest opportunity, perhaps ironically, to learn about and nurture who *you* are. In a sense, you can use your relationships with men to help you get clearer about what you think and feel about sex and love and friendship. Your relationships with men can help you find, not lose, your identity. It's not that sex can't muck things up. The average single male confronted with an attractive female will not, perhaps, have checkers and philosophic talk on his mind for a Saturday night date. And, sadly, there are still women whose self-esteem is low enough to make them think they have to be available to men who want nothing more from them than sex — men who Harry says know what women are good for. Sex charges our lives in unpredictable ways. It can wildly distort our sense of self by making us think that how someone reacts to us sexually is the true measure of our self-worth. It can make a mess of things more quickly than any other urge we feel. Because we tend to embrace it with feeling and invest it with meaning, sex can, of course, be wonderful, too — a route to pleasure and intimacy you can't experience in any other way. But, as wonderful as it can be, sex on its own is never a good basis on which to make long-term decisions about a man, and it's certainly not enough to fuel a marriage.

Because sex is so highly charged, making sense of it takes a special ability to see yourself objectively. Part of the problem is that for many women romance, sex, companionship, and love blur into one another. The dynamics that exist between you and that important man in your life are going to be complex: they'll reflect what each of you brings to the other, and a lot of what you bring is unconscious. You need to be aware of what underlies those dynamics.

Of course, it's not only women who become disillusioned with the men they choose in the heat of romance. Men just as frequently enter relationships wearing blinders. When Mike met Hannah, he felt he'd found his perfect mate. Born in Japan, Hannah was raised to be a caretaker of men. Her meals, the way she made herself beautiful for Mike, meant that his daily homecomings from the office led to romantic evenings of good food and sex. But when Hannah had a child, she had less time to give to Mike. Now she wanted him to run errands and help with the cooking and baby-tending. She also wanted him to participate in their shared life in ways not directly connected with the baby: she wanted to talk to him about her feelings and hopes for the future. But all of this wasn't in the contract Mike felt he entered into when he married Hannah. He wanted his old sexual and romantic playmate back; the abrupt shift into a world full of diapers and late-night feedings and new priorities threw him. Mike couldn't help feeling that Hannah had somehow violated the rules. He simply wasn't prepared for a "real" woman — and mother — to emerge from the pretty, subservient girl he thought he'd married.

Unfortunately, you can expect a similar response from many men. It isn't that Mike didn't have to put up with what for anyone would be some unwelcome new realities — it's no fun getting three hours of sleep a night — but his response was partly to blame Hannah for not keeping up her end of what he unconsciously saw as their bargain: to serve him. When, like Hannah, women begin to assert their "personhood," as it is the goal of this book to help you do, the men in their lives often feel confused and betrayed by the changes women begin to insist on. This can make us feel, for the moment, guilty for wanting to change. Asserting ourselves may suddenly seem wrong — aren't the men in our lives making it clear that we're hurting them?

What we don't appreciate when we fall into this way of thinking is the strength of the man's unconscious agenda: his expectations usually don't include the prospect of our changing. In short, we have to accept that learning to assert ourselves, learning to be ourselves, with men may, on some level, terrify them.

The unacknowledged agendas men *and* women bring to relationships can take many forms. Like Mike, a man may be looking for a playmate. Some men look for Mommy, just as some women look for Daddy. Growth rates vary: you may be growing faster than he is, becoming more open to trying new alternatives in your life, which means at least one of you is going to feel resentment. It may be that both of you are growing, but you're growing apart. It may be that your own dream of a relationship of peers — "friends and lovers" — is so strong that it's blinded you to the fact that your man doesn't share that dream; he may be after someone who'll devote her life to him with no thought for herself. When you both finally wake up from your dreams, reality can be pretty tough to take. You may wonder to yourself, "Where was I, anyway?"

Love doesn't have to be blind, and it doesn't have to come at the expense of either of your identities. I can tell you from my own experience and from having witnessed so many other women and couples that you *can* be friends and lovers with a man. It takes the same careful consciousness we've been talking about and developing all along: the consciousness that you're "enough" with or without a man. It also takes being alert to what each of you say you want and what may be your more hidden agendas. And it takes, perhaps most of all, enough self-respect to select a man whom you see as an equal — not someone "superior," whom you need to look up to, and not one of the walking wounded, an inadequate male you are going to "help." Neither is capable of offering you true friendship. Both types of man are chosen for their roles. Neither is a full, rounded being, which means that neither can offer or receive full, rounded love.

You don't have to be paranoid about control to be able to hold back a piece of yourself for yourself — which, as you'll see later on, is another prerequisite for true, balanced love. And you don't have to fear becoming a dishrag to give of yourself in a relationship. You can share intimately with a man without either of you losing your identity or essence.

How do you learn to do this? As always, first you have to identify what's going on in your life right now, look at what kind of relationship you're currently in, and then decide whether it is a sharing partnership or has the potential of becoming one. That's our task right now: to identify some of your current relationship dynamics to see which, if any, may be holding you back from being yourself — and from sharing with your partner — as fully, consciously, and responsibly as you can, so that you are both rewarded with an adult and mutually satisfying relationship.

We will look at four basic relationship scenarios here. You may recognize your own relationship or see it as a variation of one of these models.

■■■■■■■■■■■■■

Relationship Scenarios

1. Big Parent/Little Child

2. The Hidden Agenda

3. One Grows, the Other Doesn't

4. Friends and Lovers

Something in this list may immediately ring a bell for you. But as you read through the stories that illustrate each of these scenarios, you may also find yourself denying that you're in the painful ones, simply because accepting that you're in one of these relationships *is* so painful. However, I can promise that if you find that you're trapped in one of the three lopsided relationships (scenario 1, 2, or 3), you do have the power to change it. We get into relationships for complicated reasons. We're often responding to early-childhood instructions that, while they may be completely inappropriate today, still haunt and direct us. I can't stress enough that our goal here isn't to tear your present life and relationships down or to lay blame on you or anyone else. It's merely to awaken you to what's really going on in your life so that you can be in a better position to decide what you would like to do to improve it. But enough preliminaries. Take a look at the following scenarios for yourself and see what fits.

1. Big Parent/Little Child

Marriages based on a Big Parent/Little Child relationship can work for a long time and might even appear to be perfectly good ones, too. As long as (for example) Daddy stays Daddy and Little Girl agrees to stay Little Girl, the game can continue. But beneath the surface, Daddy usually grows to resent the demands placed on him and Little Girl usually grows to resent her lack of power. Lopsided relationships like this are tenuous because they rely on an unhealthy alliance and on both partners' acceptance of the status — and stalemate — of their roles. The alliance requires that neither partner change or grow.

If you're determined to act out a Little Child role, you may choose either a "good" or a "bad" parent. Which type of parent you are drawn to usually depends on your past. Since love is an acquired taste (we attach the label "love" to whatever we learned as children "love" meant), we typically select someone who reminds us of the parent to whom we bonded most strongly — or to whom we had the most trouble bonding.

All too many battered wives play the Little Girl role to the brutal Daddy played by their husbands. This almost always is a repetition of the relationship the woman knew with her father or father figure — a relationship she feels compelled to replay now because, dangerous as it was, it was the closest thing to love she ever knew. As terrible as it was, it was better than being neglected entirely, better than being left alone.

Roles can, of course, be reversed: the wife can play the Mommy, having final say over everything in her married life, reducing her Little Boy husband to complete subservience (although each partner may, and typically does, deny those roles). Sometimes this is handled very subtly: Big Momma isn't always brassy or castrating: she can play on his guilt or whine to get her way. She may be the "poor me" complainer who, through a show of sickness or weakness, is actually very effectively manipulating her husband to do exactly what she wants him to do. She may play the fainting bride, but she's the one calling the shots.

However, there are no real villains even in these scenarios, as tempting as it may be to want to assign blame. Even the one who appears to win really isn't winning. What has a Big Momma or a Big Daddy actually won except the willing acquiescence of someone who's equally bound to a script? There's rarely any true communication between a man and a woman in a parent/child relationship: each person is too busy playing out his or her role.

Often they may trade roles with each other for a time, and then revert. What they never do, however, is grow. Since both partners are trapped in their roles, neither can become a fully developed human being. Neither is really listened to or allowed to express him- or herself or even begin to grow.

If you're in this type of relationship, you need the help this book has been offering perhaps most of all. When your view of yourself is limited to playing a role, it means you're depending on the dynamics of that role for identity, rather than trusting that you've got the wherewithal to meet life spontaneously, flexibly. People adhere to roles because they feel they need to be armed with an artificial battery of personality traits without which they're convinced they couldn't survive. Not that there aren't reasons you may have developed this belief that you need to be armed: we don't choose our roles arbitrarily. There are always reasons for clinging to our beliefs, even the most negative and self-destructive of them, and we need to be compassionate about them if we're to have a chance of replacing them with something healthier. All of the couples you meet in this chapter give us lessons in learning that compassion: in identifying with one or more of these people, you may be able to direct some of that compassion toward yourself.

Dan and Carol both came from difficult backgrounds. Both grew up in broken homes and neither really knew how a healthy marriage was supposed to work. Dan's mother died when he was two, and his father left him in the care of two maiden aunts; he never felt any spontaneous love from any parental figure as a child, and he grew up lonely and isolated. Carol's father died when she was eight, leaving Carol, her mother, and an older sister destitute. They ran a small grocery store, and all Carol remembers of her childhood was how hard she had to work. She never had a girlhood in any normal sense; she never went out on dates because she had to mind the store. School functions, from dances to football games, were not permitted as excuses by her mother for not working. Carol became a tough woman, devoid of easy warmth, but she was reliable, industrious, and competent at any job she took on. She and Dan met in a business course in a local community college. Carol was the motivated one; Dan was, even then, the follower. They clicked almost immediately: each sensed that he or she could complete the other. Unfortunately, what they were completing were each other's neurotic needs. Carol needed to dominate someone the way she'd felt dominated by her mother throughout her childhood; Dan needed to be told what to do by some stand-in for the parents he never had.

It was uncomfortable to visit Carol and Dan the rare times they socialized or had anyone over to dinner. There was often a feeling of tension. Carol looked for opportunities to tell guests how impractical and disorganized Dan was: "What do you think of a man who doesn't hang up his clothes?" she'd say. "My other children are growing up. Not Dan — he'll be my child forever." Dan, meanwhile, smiled sheepishly, continually going to the kitchen to refill glasses, praising his wife for how good the canapés were. He wanted to please. Carol gave structure to his life. He needed her. But Carol responded to his praise by mocking him. While you could tell she loved him, there was something beneath that love that caused the tension, something inescapable: she held him in some contempt. Their game was beginning to wear a little thin.

When Carol came for therapy, she did so because she had had a skiing accident and was depressed by her husband's sudden lack of attention and help. She was baffled: "Dan was always at my heels like a puppy dog before. Now he's disappeared!" She'd call him at the office and plead with him to come home, do the grocery shopping, help with the kids. She was in pain and she couldn't do all these things herself. But it was as if Dan didn't want to play anymore. Now that Carol couldn't play his mother because she was laid up in bed, Dan seemed to respond by sulking like a little boy disappointed in his parents. All Carol could see was that Dan had become more of an irresponsible brat than ever. "Why can't he take charge?" she asked me. I knew this was what Carol thought she wanted, but she herself had engineered a different kind of relationship with Dan. She had to awaken to the real dynamics between them.

When she began to talk about her childhood, she let in a little light. Carol opened up about how lonely she'd felt as a girl, how impossible it seemed that she'd ever find love anywhere. "I knew the only way out was through work," she said, "so I worked like the devil. I made money — and then, well, there was Dan." She paused for a moment. "Dan gave me so much attention, right from the start. It was like I was suddenly being offered what I'd missed my whole girlhood: someone who would listen to me, love me, pay attention to me, look up to me. Dan was a little younger than I and thought I was worldly. I took over the relationship, and he seemed happy about it. I guess we both were."

Carol had in fact found exactly the man she was looking for: she discovered someone who would give her control over both their lives. Dan was a man who she felt couldn't get along without her; she was deeply convinced that she was better than he was at functioning in the world, and she derived satisfaction from that. Unconsciously, she felt she was finally getting back at her controlling mother. When she began, in therapy, slowly to realize that she was the one who had set the dynamic of their relationship — even if Dan was a willing party to the crime —

she realized that she couldn't blame Dan for not suddenly changing now that she needed him to. That wasn't the role she picked him for, and it wasn't the role he accepted. She was supposed to be the caretaker, not he. Dan simply wasn't prepared for her as a helpless girl; it wasn't in their script.

There's every chance Dan and Carol's marriage can survive if they understand the contract they've made with each other and if they agree to change it. It is too bad that we tend to deal with these issues only when a crisis occurs: it took Carol's accident for their problems to surface. But, ultimately, we can be grateful for whatever catalysts help to bring the real issues up for us. When we've identified what's really going on, we at least have the chance of changing it.

Part of what's really going on when we make this kind of hidden contract with another person to fulfill certain roles is that we're unconsciously agreeing to exist in a state of fear — a fear of *self*. When you begin to wake up to your ability to meet life more openly and flexibly — which you will, as you learn to take full responsibility for your life — your need for these roles will become less urgent. Obviously that's a goal of this book, to help with that awakening. Your very quest for self-reliance ensures that you'll start to question much of your reflexive behavior, including role-playing.

However, because we've depended for so long on the rewards of role-playing, it's not easy to extract ourselves from our contracts. Respecting the reasons we get into those contracts can help us to appreciate their power and become clearer about what we need to do to get out of them.

It's not uncommon for a woman like Carol to want to act out her frustration with Dan by betraying him with a "real man." It's also not uncommon for a man to take a lover when he sees his wife in a mother role. If a man turns his wife into his mother, he frequently won't want to sleep with her; the incest taboo is so strong that he often looks outside the marriage for sex. Again, this comes from following deeply ingrained scripts that can't be cast aside until you've awakened to the fact that they're there.

If you're in a Big Parent/Little Child marriage or relationship, you're more than likely playing out some scripts with very deep roots. This book can't help you rid yourself of these scripts completely, but it can aid you in becoming more aware that you might be in their grip. If a bell is striking (however distantly) that you might be in this kind of relationship, take that as a sign that you need to explore things further. Therapy will help you with that exploration, but so will participating in the quest for self you've already begun simply by following the exercises in this book.

2. The Hidden Agenda

One very common and painful trap many men and women fall into when they get married is that they marry the idea of marriage, they don't really marry a human being at all. Or they may marry the life-style certain marriages make possible, with no real thought to the person attached to it. Phyllis and Jay offer a good example.

Phyllis, twenty-three years old, is a pretty and confident woman from a secure and well-to-do family. Her parents doted on her — she was an only child — and she grew up with the idea that the world was her oyster. She met Jay, twenty-seven and just out of law school, on a beach in Hawaii. Phyllis had just graduated from college and her parents gave her the trip as a graduation present; Jay had just passed his bar exam and used a chunk of his savings to treat himself to a "congratulations" gift. One look at each other, and Phyllis and Jay fell in love. The chemistry was terrific. They both felt on top of the world now that they'd gotten through school, and the balmy Hawaiian evening breezes didn't hurt either. Only a few days into their romance, Phyllis decided Jay was the one. He was handsome and had all the right credentials (undergraduate at Stanford; Harvard Law). He was right out of her girlhood picture of the perfect match. Jay was obviously taken with Phyllis too, and when they discovered they both had plans to move to New York, the idea hit them both simultaneously: they were so much in love, why not live together?

That's exactly what they did. Only Phyllis had a not-so-hidden agenda. From the first week of living together, she began to apply pressure; her parents were not pleased that she was living with a man and were badgering her to get married. Jay was just starting his practice at a small firm, and wouldn't it help his career to have a wife? What Phyllis managed to do was maneuver Jay into marriage — not that he might not have come to want it on his own, but Phyllis, Jay later realized, was doing the pushing. Jay, who came to me for advice once he began to realize what was going on, is now able to see Phyllis's motivations more clearly: "Once we got married," he said, "Phyllis began the same pressure techniques about moving out of New York — about how it would do my career good to have an impressive house in the suburbs, and what if we had kids — we couldn't bring kids up in New York. . . . I tried to explain that I wasn't making enough money yet to buy a house, I'd only just started my practice. But it was like she didn't hear me. And then it clicked: she'd never really listened to me about anything. She was so full of her own agendas and fantasies about what she wanted her marriage to be like, that it was like I didn't exist at all except as a kind of prop. She'd married the marriage, she hadn't married me."

Phyllis was trying to force Jay into her own dream with-out consulting him. And yet she had so much denial about this, she was baffled at any suggestion that she was trying to control Jay and their marriage. Jay says whenever he tried to bring it up, she'd pout and say, "But I'm only doing what's best for both of us!" Phyllis and Jay face some difficult days ahead: she has to awaken to the fact that marriage means a commitment to an actual person, not an idea, and he has to face the possibility that once she does finally see him, they may each have second thoughts about their relationship. There's also no guar-antee that Phyllis will wake up to Jay's reality; if she doesn't, Jay will have to decide whether he wants to con-tinue in the marriage.

The problem Jay and Phyllis illustrate is very common. Some partners are really attracted to life-styles, not to other people. Someone's wealth, prestige, connections, family — there are any number of lures we may fall for other than the actual man. People married to this kind of fantasy aren't really married at all; they've simply bought into an idea of marriage without any sense that there's an actual breathing, fallible human being attached. Waking up to the fact that you're in a myth, not a mar-riage, can be painful: it means giving up some simplistic ideas about what you thought marriage meant, and it may mean having to get to know the man you've married for the first time — maybe years after you said "I do."

But how does this relate to our message of self-reliance? It's interesting that even a woman like Phyllis, who ap-pears to know exactly what she wants, who appears to be self-reliant at least insofar as she makes no secret about what her desires are and then exerts her will to fill them — even this woman is often deeply battling the same *fear of self* we've met in women who are far less assertive. The life plan Phyllis attempted to cling to so fiercely wasn't, really, her own: she was responding to a *received* notion of happiness, not one she had created for herself. It takes deep self-trust to pursue your own vision of fulfillment. And it's exactly our task here to find ways to develop that trust. The value of looking at Phyllis's predicament isn't in judging her inability to see and accept her husband and her life for what they really are. It's in allowing her story to nudge us into recognizing ways we may be similarly trapping ourselves. You can't get out of a trap until you see how it works: that's the point of what we're exploring in this and every other story in this chapter.

3. *One Grows, the Other Doesn't*

Joyce and Howard went through a very rocky transition period that illustrates this "one grows, the other doesn't" scenario. Joyce was the quintessential dutiful daughter throughout childhood: she is a sweet-natured Midwesterner who grew up in a strict religious household where Daddy was king and Mommy deferred to him in every way. Joyce fell in love with and married Howard. He wasn't religious in the same ways her parents were, for which she was grateful; in fact, she felt she'd rebelled healthily against her background by getting out from under her strict moral upbringing. But in every other way, Howard reflected her father — Joyce just didn't see it. Howard was the one who decided everything in their lives. Howard implicitly expected Joyce to follow the marriage vows, to "love, honor, and *obey*."

"I don't know when I began realizing I was becoming my mother," Joyce says. "Maybe I do remember. It seems silly, but I was passing this trendy T-shirt store and I saw this shirt with a cartoon of a woman's agonized face and the caption, 'Oh no, I've become my mother!' I thought it was a silly T-shirt, but for some reason I couldn't get it out of my mind. When I got home and started cooking dinner for Howard — he always wanted to eat at a certain time and threw a fit if we were even a few minutes late sitting down at the table — I got this vivid picture of my mother stirring pots in our kitchen and the feeling of tension I always had before Daddy came home. My mother would snap at me to set the table and make sure I was cleaned up and ready for Daddy. Daddy, Daddy — everything revolved around him! Suddenly I realized why that T-shirt had riveted me. I had become my mother! I was acting the same way, waiting for Howard to come home, trying to get everything ready so he wouldn't be mad at me. Suddenly I felt angry."

Joyce tried to talk to Howard that night about her feelings, about how she felt a little trapped by their life. Howard looked at her blankly. He had no idea what she was talking about. "I realized in that moment that Howard and I had never developed a real vocabulary to talk about feelings. He really didn't know what was bothering me." Howard wondered if she needed more money for household expenses (he controlled the checkbook). Or was her job the problem, he wondered? Maybe she should find another. He couldn't grasp anything other than the concrete facts of life. She had a husband, home, child, and job — what more could she want? The notion that Joyce might feel emotionally trapped didn't register. "I remember he finally patted me on the head, as if he were my father, and asked me if it was that time of the month. 'Take an aspirin,' he told me. 'You'll feel better in the morning.' " Joyce pauses to take a deep breath. "I looked at him as if for the first time. It was frightening. I realized there was a whole part of me Howard didn't even know existed. But how could he? I hadn't allowed myself to see who I really was."

Joyce began to think about herself differently from that

day on. She had the urge to do something to reclaim her life. She began to make a mental list; then, when the list grew too long, she wrote it down. It was a list of things she knew she had to bring up with Howard. "I don't want to give you my check every week" was one item. "I want my own checkbook." She had to drum up some courage to write the next: "I don't want to have sex just because you want to." Others followed more quickly: "I want to spend time with friends without your permission or having you guilt-trip me." Joyce suddenly realized what she wanted to tell Howard *and* herself: "I want to be a grown-up."

It wasn't easy actually to talk to Howard about the items on her list, but Joyce made herself do it anyway. "It was painful," she says. "I could tell Howard didn't understand what was going on. He'd say, looking hurt, 'Don't I take care of you? Don't I give you everything you need?' And I'd try to explain that that wasn't the point. I needed to have a voice in our lives — in my life. I needed to be taken seriously. I needed to have a life of my own."

To Howard's credit, it was he who originally came to see me. He loved Joyce, and although it was difficult for him to accept the changes in her, he wanted to try. Joyce and Howard are still working with the new Joyce. What Howard is slowly realizing is that there has to be a new Howard, too, at least if the marriage is to continue. It's not easy. "Sometimes I find myself blaming Howard for everything," Joyce says, "but then I realize that's not fair. I mean, he married the little Joyce who'd grown up in her domineering father's household. Now he finds he's getting an independent woman, someone he hadn't bargained for. But that's who I am. And that's who he'll have to accept."

Growth is never easy. We grow by passing through fear, by extending ourselves beyond what we used to think we were capable of. If you identify with the One Grows, the Other Doesn't model and you feel yourself to be the emerging adult, be aware that you will continue to face fear and that the metamorphosis you're undergoing probably will have moments of pain and relapse into old behaviors. But that doesn't mean you can't start growing again and remain conscious that you're changing for the better. Don't give in to what I know will be the frequent temptations to blame him or just to stop and give up. The growth you're experiencing is the most wonderful thing in the world: you *deserve* to become all you can be; you deserve the increasing sense of self-reliance you're developing. If your partner is feeling insecure, feeling you are growing away from him, it is important that you be clear about your own path; don't blame him for not understanding or for trying to hold you back. Remember that no one can hold you back from growth but yourself. Try to engage him in your growth; a dividend may be that he'll grow, too.

4. Friends and Lovers

Barry and Norma are a great example of this happy category. Their strongest suit as a couple is that they actually talk to each other. They don't let themselves react in the reflexive ways that mean your tape is running but your mind isn't. As Norma describes it, "When I start to feel angry about something, I wait for a minute to see if it's something really important or if it's just a mood, a bad time of the month, or something trivial. If it isn't any of those things, I talk about it." When most couples hear about premarital contracts or about the kind of entrance-and-exit agreement Barry and Norma drew up between them, they wince: it sounds like bringing boardroom methods into the bedroom. But Barry and Norma say they have made the terms of their relationship explicit not because they don't care about each other, but precisely because they do.

"What we're really doing is playing to each of our strengths," says Norma. "We're each very open people, and it's been pretty much no-holds-barred about what happened to us in our pasts — we really don't have any secrets from one another. One thing we didn't want either of us to go through was the kind of messy and painful breakup we'd seen our friends go through. It's not that we're planning to part; in fact, I have every expectation that we'll spend the rest of our lives together. But we're both realistic enough to know that life can change unpredictably, and while we're as loving as we can be, we want to make sure we protect ourselves, whatever happens in the future." This attitude isn't an easy one to adopt. We have such strong prejudices about what romantic love should be like: we should be swept off our feet and stay swept off. But, as you undoubtedly know from your own experience, people have a way of coming down to earth. And sometimes the landing isn't an easy one. Norma and Barry don't want their lives to fall apart if they can help it, so they have tried to cover all bases.

"We were clear at the start about each of us having our own money," said Norma. "We've come to some mutual ground rules about raising our kids — we've got two boys, five and eight — and we've already decided how much of each of our incomes will be put away for their college educations. We've talked over some other issues that a lot of other couples find difficult to face — like monogamy. I wanted to make it clear to Barry that my commitment to him was exclusive, and I wanted to hear from him that his commitment to me was exclusive, too, before I could share my life with him. Not all of this is written down! I mean, so much of the emotional ground rules can't really be put into a partnership agreement,"

Norma laughs. "But the financial details can be written down, and they are. If for some reason we have to split, neither of us will be raked over the coals by the other's lawyer." Norma says that she knows this might make them seem awfully cold and cynical. "But people make wills, don't they? I mean, it seems just as shortsighted not to plan for a divorce as it is not to plan for the inescapable fact that nobody get off this planet alive! That's the practical spirit we try to bring to our marriage. And far from making us love each other less, we find we love each other more. We respect each other, and we've proven it by ironing out some basic issues between us, some of them legally."

Barry says it succinctly: "Norma is my best friend. That's what makes our marriage work. We like each other." It's amazing how many men and women who are attracted to each other never find out whether or not they like each other. You may swoon at his bedroom eyes, one glance from him across the room may make your knees weak, but does he pick up after himself? Is he rude? Is he honest? Does he enjoy doing any of the things you enjoy doing? Or, even if he doesn't, will he respect the fact that you like doing things on your own? There are any number of questions you don't want to consider at that heady moment of attraction, but unfortunately they're the questions you've got to consider if anything longer than a brief affair is going to work.

Marriage is not a brief affair. When you approach it with a "Love conquers all!" attitude, you generally find pretty quickly that romantic love doesn't conquer much of anything — except your emotions for a night or two. Marriage for a self-reliant woman is a pact not agreed to lightly. The kind of careful attention to each other's fears, desires, and needs that Barry and Norma have been able to bring to their marriage can only exist when each partner feels strong enough to ask for and give what each deems to be important. This means, first of all, becoming *clear* about what you want, feeling that you *deserve* what you want, and then being capable of accepting the responsibilities entailed in *getting* what you want: another statement of our overall goal in this book.

As you become stronger in this process, you'll find that your very vocabulary will change. Perhaps the most essential component of a good marriage is the ability to say what you mean — and to hear what your partner is telling you. It's amazing how fear of self can block both abilities. There are, however, certain hallmarks of good communication between a man and woman that we can identify and that you can work toward. Let's explore them now.

■■■■■■■■■■■■■■

Couple Talk: Sharpening Communication Skills

The first rule of good communication skills is the simplest: *Say what you mean.* Sometimes through fear or the belief that he won't understand something if you say it in your own terms — that you have to hint or translate in order to get your desires across — you end up smothering what you want to say so that it never really gets said. Obviously, this will only make things more muddled. Next time you want to bring up a point with your lover or husband, use the following five communication tactics. They will help you get your point across and give you an opportunity to tell him who you are and what you want without sending him sulking out of the room.

1. State what you want instead of hinting at it.

This is a variation on our general rule to say what you mean. Prepare what you want to say in the simplest terms.

This will help you to be clear about what you want as well as making things clear to him.

2. Don't accuse.

Sometimes when we want to bring something up, we drum up courage by saying something like, "I know you're not going to like this — you never do — but . . .," or, as a prologue to talking about how you might like to hire some part-time help with the housework, "You always criticize me in public for not being a good housekeeper, and you know I work and have to take care of the kids . . ." We sometimes take a defensive stand before we've even given him a chance to respond. Remember our "Think aikido" emotional fitness tip? Apply it here. Don't get your guns ready. All you're doing is saying something you feel. You have that right, and you don't have to attack to exercise it.

3. Use "I" statements.

Make it clear that you're saying something from your point of view and not making sweeping statements of fact. It's not "Every other woman has what I want," but "I really feel the need for this, and I believe I have the right to it." Tell things from your personal point of view: make it explicit that you've thought this through and that neither of you has to make a judgment about it. It's neither right nor wrong, it's what you feel.

4. Don't use emotionally charged words to make your point.

Don't think that by making him feel guilty or angry or hurt you'll be gaining points: things that hurt or rile someone up usually make matters worse. Keep your tone neutral. "You're a terrible person. How could you do something so horrible? Your mother is destroying our relationship" can be better expressed by "It hurts me when you behave that way. Do you want me to be hurt?" or "I don't feel you acted appropriately, and it seems others didn't feel you did either. Do you care?" or "You and I are allowing your mother to come between us. Can we talk about changing that?"

5. Find out whether he's willing to discuss the issue before you launch into it.

If he's so defensive that you can't get past his brick wall, take time out. This is not the time to try to persuade him. Do, however, clearly acknowledge that his unwillingness to talk about the issue is creating distance between you. And that you will need to talk about it soon. For example: "It's obvious from your reaction that you don't want to talk about your mother. I'll drop it for now, but I need you to know that not talking about it makes me feel farther away from you, so please think about talking about it soon."

These suggestions may sound as if they'll only work in an ideal world, but, trust me, they will work right here and now. Be clear; be kind; be honest. Those are the watchwords of good communication. They may sound like the same old eternal verities, but they are very useful guides to communicating with the man in your life. That's why we call them eternal verities: they're true.

Launching into a series of tips about good communication isn't as much a departure from our theme of self-reliance as you may at first think. It's only by communicating the new self you're developing through becoming self-reliant that you can begin to have an impact on your relationships. The sense of true communion that grows from communicating honestly and compassionately with a mate not only reinforces the satisfaction of that union, but it reinforces your own sense of personal power. Your very relationship can become an arena in which you assert your wants and needs effectively in a way that will not only get what you want for yourself, but will allow your mate to be a participant, not an adversary, in your life.

Self-reliance is really at the root of being able to communicate effectively and lovingly. Feeling the strength of self that, for example, Norma feels with Barry, leads to a willingness to meet your partner fully, openly, with your whole self. The sense of commitment this leads to can be extraordinary — a commitment that doesn't stifle who either of you is, but rather provides common, fertile ground for your growth, together and singly. Developing commitment based on the self-reliance of both partners is so rewarding and important — and rare — that it deserves to be looked at more closely.

■ ■ ■ ■ ■ ■ ■ ■ ■ ■ ■ ■ ■ ■

Commitment

First, permit me to express a strong — and, you may think, old-fashioned — bias. Living with a man is usually a mistake if you're not married. Not because you're "living in sin" — that's a private matter that has nothing to do with my opinion. It's usually a mistake for some very practical reasons, and I've seen too many women get hurt not to feel compelled to tell you what I perceive those reasons to be.

It is tragically common for women to assume that the men with whom they get involved have the same investment in the relationship that they do. The sense of commitment we've just talked about isn't something that happens overnight, and yet, in our ache for it, women often see it when it isn't there. Marriage is a testament to *each* partner's commitment to making their relationship work. It is a pledge to honor and respect each other. Women devalue themselves when they trade themselves off for some fantasy of intimacy or commitment. This is often what happens when a woman falls in love and gives herself to a man without benefit of the legal protection of marriage. And when such relationships end, it is just like a divorce — with the same suffering and feelings of abandonment and isolation to be worked through — except there is no legal redress. You already know that I want you to value yourself highly; I want you to consider your own needs on a par with others'. It is imperative, for all the reasons we've explored so far, that you learn to take care of yourself. It's not that you shouldn't have relationships with men before deciding to get married, but don't confuse sexual electricity with commitment. Realize that relationships do end, and protect yourself from getting badly hurt. If he's not willing to make the commitment of marriage, don't think he'll come around eventually just because you're ready for it.

A public declaration is for better or worse. Living together without that public declaration too often is just for "bed her." Don't end up with all the emotional work of marriage but none of the protection.

Let's say, however, that you've both got that sense of commitment. Is this an invitation to give your life totally to him?

Perhaps the most important advice I can pass on about being happy, whether in or out of marriage, is this: *Save a piece of yourself for yourself.* Never give all of you away. Continue to have friends, continue to see your family, to have money of your own. Continue your school or career plans. Consider going away on your own every so often, if only for a day. Remember our emotional fitness exercises: practice these even now, even in the context of the marriage you've always wanted for yourself. You need to be emotionally fit — capable of making your own decisions, facing challenges, being on your own — just as much when you've got what you want as you do when you're still pursuing it. In fact, saving a piece of yourself for yourself is even *more* important when you're in a marriage or relationship. You won't have anything to give if you don't replenish the stock — the stock of *who you are.* See yourself as an independent being, not as an adjunct or a piece of the jigsaw puzzle of his life. That's the attitude that engenders healthy commitment, not unhealthy dependency.

Happiness does not — cannot — depend on anyone outside yourself. This isn't to say that good relationships aren't worth pursuing: of course they are. As we've seen (and as you undoubtedly know), there are wonderful rewards to be found in intimate relationships. But whether or not you happen to be reaping those rewards right now, you can still have a productive and satisfying life. If there's a secret to happiness, we find it when we learn to define what happiness means to each of us, *alone,* and then make an effort, whether it ends up in success or not, to achieve it. Happiness comes in that effort, that self-propulsion toward true self-reliance, even more than in its achievement.

7

■■■■■■■■■■■■■■

Without Him . . .

■■■■■■■■■■■■■■■■■

WHEN Jessica walked into my office, I thought I was seeing a real-life re-creation of Maude from the film *Harold and Maude*. Adorable, full of life, carefully made up, this au courant seventy-year-old could have taught much younger women how to dress and carry themselves. It was inspiring just to look at her.

So why was she so miserable? She hadn't sat down before the first tears fell. She began simply: "He's gone." She wiped her eyes. "He's left me for another woman."

"Oh, dear," I said. "Had you been married a long time?"

"Oh, no, we never married," she said. "It's just that he decided he wanted to have a family. He's only thirty-nine, you see."

Thirty-nine! Jessica had become even more inspiring. I asked her to tell me more. "He said he loved me and he always would, but he had to go on. And I can't help feeling my life is ruined!" Jessica had been married for forty years when her first husband died; a few years later she met

Joe. Joe was a handyman who worked in the neighborhood. He was then in his mid-thirties and he'd never married. Jessica had needed help with the house now that her husband was gone; Joe obliged. She would make him meals, invite him over to watch television. "We knew we were on the same wavelength from the start," said Jessica. "I also knew that I hadn't felt this way toward any man since my husband." It turned out Joe felt strongly about Jessica, too. After a late supper and an old, romantic movie on TV, Joe let Jessica know that he didn't want to go home. They spent the night together — and many nights thereafter. Soon Joe all but lived with Jessica. She gave him a room in her large house, and their life together was comfortable and loving. But then, as Jessica said, "He told me he had to go. How could I begrudge him another woman?" she asked tearfully. "If he wants to have children, he has a right to go." But she felt devastated. She also said she felt like a fool. "I'm a seventy-year-old woman! Was I crazy to get involved with someone so much younger?"

I looked at Jessica — this vibrant seventy-year-old woman who had just had a relationship with a man more than thirty years her junior — with some awe. I saw her very differently from the way she saw herself. Of course she was upset at the end of a love affair. Who isn't? But she needed to see what she had done for herself: she had made herself into an exciting, alive, desirable woman long past the cut-off point most women feel they reach when they get older. The risk that Joe would go had always been there; it was there from the first moment she met him. It's a risk that exists for any of us who fall in love. And the risk that we'll be devastated heightens considerably when we become dependent on a man. But Jessica had so much to feel good about! She had demonstrated that she was able to turn her life around once; why not turn it around again? Not that she had to run around seeking a thirty-nine-year-old replacement for Joe, but she had every reason to become receptive to life once again. She was certainly entitled to her feelings of loss right now. It might, indeed, take some time for her to get over Joe. But she had no reason to blame herself for being too old. She deserved to realize two things: she obviously wasn't too old — look at what happened with Joe! — and she could bring the same zest she'd brought to her relationship with Joe to every other aspect of her life. If I had closed my eyes and listened to her, Jessica could have been a woman of any age. Any woman would have identified with her feelings. And it was clear to me that she had every reason to be optimistic about her life — the same as any other woman, no matter what her age. She could be happy with or without a man.

Jessica is a dramatic example of how we can go a long way toward living self-reliantly — bucking convention when we know it means living a more satisfying life — and yet come to certain blocks nonetheless. You may find that your feeling of self-reliance has limits. As much as we come to believe that we have the right to live and love as we please, sometimes this self-confidence can prove itself to be incomplete — and when it falters, we may start to doubt *everything* about ourselves. Much of Jessica's life was, to me, a model of believing in and nurturing her own personal power, and yet she could see none of this about herself when Joe left her. Love was such a charged state that it awoke a host of old fears and dependencies. It would take some healing for her to regain her original sense of herself as vital, independent, and desirable *on her own*.

The point here is to acknowledge that just because we may suffer disappointments in love doesn't mean we have to feel as if we've lost all power to direct our lives satisfyingly — much as that may be the way we feel at the time a love relationship ends. Other women have responded to the problem of being left differently from Jessica. The felt loss of self that's so common after divorce, for example, evokes a range of responses that can be valuable to explore to give us an idea of how to regain our self-reliance even after it has been most painfully attacked. As we've seen before, we are never more vulnerable than in love — unless it's when we feel love has been withdrawn. Look at the following women's experience with that withdrawal of love to see how they struggled to regain their selfhood. As a result, you will understand more about your own struggle for selfhood after disappointment in love. You'll see that you still have an enormous range of options in marriage or out of it — options to be who *you* want to be.

■■■■■■■■■■■■■■■

Life Before and After Divorce: Weighing Options

Sharon is a forty-year-old single mother with two young children, a boy of ten and a girl of seven. She'd played the conventional script well: married to a doctor, she lived in a nice suburban home in a community chosen for its good schools and convenient proximity to the city. Sharon enjoyed being a mother, but when her kids were both old enough to be in school, she felt the need to get involved in something new. She'd had some background as a book editor, and she decided to see what she might be able to do with it now after some years out of the business. She was delighted to connect with a good publishing house quickly: they needed a freelance editor, which, with her time schedule, worked out well. Sharon's husband wasn't thrilled about her working. Although he'd never explicitly said he thought "a woman's place was in the kitchen" — he was too much of a "liberal" to say that — he was obviously uncomfortable that Sharon was dividing her time between home and work. The situation, from her husband's point of view, worsened when Sharon was given a promotion — and asked to work full-time. Now Sharon joined the ranks of those women who work two shifts a day: taking care of the house and the kids, as expected by her husband, and putting in full, long days at the office.

"My husband was not happy when I had to work late, to put it mildly. He said it was interfering with our life at home. But what he really meant was that it was interfering with his own conception of what a wife was supposed to do. He finally came out and said that he thought his work was more important than mine, and that I should accommodate his wishes. I mean, he was a doctor, saving people's lives — wasn't that important enough to make me sacrifice a little to make his life at home easier? He earned enough money to keep me and the kids. Why would I want to jeopardize all that by spending so much time out of the house?"

Sharon had an uncomfortable awakening. "Now that the truth was out — that he thought what he was doing was more important than the job I had, a job I loved, a job that gave me a lot of my self-esteem — I began to realize the subtle ways he'd gotten me to bend to his will in other areas. We never went on a vacation he didn't choose. We never bought an appliance he didn't okay. I couldn't, I guess, exactly blame him, since I'd unwittingly allowed this to continue — this domination of his will over mine. It was just easier that way, to give in to him. But now I started to get angry."

The more Sharon tried to express her desire for more autonomy, the more her husband withdrew. " 'You're not the woman I married,' he finally said to me. And one day I woke up realizing he wasn't the man I wanted to be married to. He kept saying my first obligation was to him and the kids, and I realized, suddenly, that my first obligation was to *me* and the kids." Sharon decided to divorce him. "My relief was so immediate and unexpected, I cried," she says. "It was like a hundred sixty-five pounds had been lifted off my shoulders."

As frightening, disruptive, and painful as divorce can be, truly acknowledging that you're unhappy and capable of having a better life on your own can be cleansing. For the first time in years, Sharon did not feel that she had to be "less" so that somebody else could be "more." For the first time in years, she could find pleasure in work without any accompanying guilt. After a long talk with her children, explaining that they could always spend as much time as they liked with their father — even living with him, if they chose — she was able to begin her new life. She knew it would be hard, especially at first, and especially with children. But they all adjusted, one day at a time. She made sure her kids felt loved, and she made an effort never to be negative about their father in front of them.

Now, divorced for five years, Sharon feels she has a full life. She sees certain men occasionally — in fact, she became very involved with one man at one point. But when she began to feel that possessive pressure from him, when he started to talk marriage so that he could take care of her, she was wary. She didn't want to fall into that trap again, and she wasn't ready, when she looked into her heart, to make that kind of commitment . . . maybe not ever. "Sometimes the old tape my mother planted in me started playing," Sharon says. " 'You're forty years old,' the tape goes, 'and you should marry the next man who asks you!' " Sharon smiles. "But I know that's not the ticket for me anymore. I grabbed at marriage before, and I nearly suffocated. I don't want to risk suffocating again. And anyway, my life is so full now. I don't need any magical cure-all for it — nothing needs fixing! I have wonderful friends, great kids. I know my kids will grow up and leave someday, and that's okay, too. I'm in pretty good financial shape. My philosophy is: I'm the person I have to go through life with, so why not make myself into somebody I enjoy?"

Sharon wonderfully illustrates how responding to your inner need to grow can pay off, even if it brings you through pain. A hard truth we've seen many times before in this book (and that you've undoubtedly faced in your life) is that growth often means having to suffer pain. Transforming your life takes courage, and deciding that you need to leave a marriage in order to further your own transformation can trigger some of your greatest, deepest fears. But allowing yourself to undergo that transformation by facing up to your particular life challenges is *always* productive — and will lead you to feelings of relief similar to those Sharon felt so vividly when she got out from under the yoke of her marriage.

Gloria, the next woman you'll meet, responded to her inner need to grow less courageously and completely; she didn't go the whole distance to transformation that Sharon allowed herself. As a result she's stuck in a way that is all too common for many other women, as you'll see.

It's not that Gloria didn't have her own awakening. She decided to divorce Stan, her husband of twenty-three years, when she finally got to a point where she couldn't stand his nagging at her. "He was like a mosquito buzzing in my ear," says Gloria. "It's a wonder I put up with him for so long. I guess I was brought up to think you didn't break up as long as your kids were growing up — and I was afraid to face life without a husband once they did grow up. But finally I knew I'd had it." Gloria had, in fact, married Stan to give her two children a father: their bi-

ological father had died early in the kids' lives. "But it
didn't work," Gloria says. "My kids never got along with
Stan. He was always criticizing anything they did —
when he wasn't criticizing me. It was a relief when I left
him!" Gloria's friends applauded her; they never knew
how she'd put up with him, either. He was cheap, anti-
social, and verbally abusive — he'd made her life miserable. "At forty-five," Gloria says, "I had a few good years
ahead of me, so divorcing Stan was the best thing I could
have done. At least that's what I thought then."

Six months after the divorce, Stan died. "I was making
a living as a practical nurse," Gloria says, "but I was just
scraping by. I couldn't help feeling, why didn't I stay one
more year? At least I could have inherited something! I
know that sounds terrible and callous, but when you put
up with a man like Stan all those years, you get to thinking you deserve something for all that trouble." Gloria
was bitter — and she no longer felt the relief of being on
her own. She suddenly felt intense loneliness.

She tried to go out and meet men, but the singles scene
embarrassed her. "I couldn't flirt with men," Gloria says.
"What was I supposed to do? I felt foolish dressing up in
sexy clothes and going out to singles bars or parties." And
yet Gloria's entire focus is now on getting a man. She is
still reacting to not getting anything from Stan's will. She
still sees any chance of security (let alone happiness) as
something bound up with whether she can find the right
man to fix it all. But when her friends introduce her to
men, she doesn't like any of them. She's locked in by her
bitterness toward Stan: she won't allow herself to trust
any man she meets. It's a painful Catch-22. She's decided
she needs a man for happiness and security, but she's so
mistrustful of every man she meets that she's effectively
blocked herself off from ever getting into a relationship.

What Gloria hasn't done is obvious — at least to us.

She hasn't made friends with herself. She hasn't taken stock of her own resources to see how much she might be able to do for herself without that magical man. She's locked into a life of misery because she's locked into warring assumptions, variations on "you can't live with him/you can't live without him." But she hasn't spent a moment really looking at herself.

Gloria's anger and bitterness block out a painful truth. She hasn't developed the self-esteem to really believe she can make it on her own. The difference between her attitude and Sharon's is simply that Gloria is reacting to her bad marriage to Stan without taking steps to replace it with anything meaningful for herself. When you do nothing but react to situations, you can't initiate anything new. You spend your life backing off, not moving toward.

Beth gives us another example of how insidiously we can sabotage ourselves by reacting instead of truly responding. After two marriages, no children, and a hysterectomy that precludes having any children in the future, Beth felt she had summarily left the world of men. What did she need a man for? she asked herself. She threw herself into her career: she got promoted steadily at the public relations firm where she worked, and she tried to make that her life. She was in touch with one ex-husband occasionally, but they maintained a safe distance. No man could truly penetrate the shell she'd built around herself. Then Martin appeared.

Martin was a client of the PR company where Beth worked, and he took to her immediately. Beth was flustered. She hadn't allowed herself to get involved with any man, and she was determined not to start now. But she hadn't banked on Martin's perseverance. "I don't know," Beth says. "It was like he could tell I was some hurt animal, that my experience with men up until now had never been good. He didn't know about my hysterectomy, of course, but it was as if he could sense I felt that I was damaged goods, and he felt compassion for me." This was intolerable to Beth. "I didn't want anyone feeling sorry for me — least of all a man!" She realizes that she started to gain weight around this time as a form of self-defense.

"I knew, or at least I must have known deep down then — this is all coming out in therapy now — that if I were fat, men wouldn't find me attractive. Specifically Martin. But even after I gained weight, Martin didn't stop calling me, inviting me out. I don't know why I just didn't firmly tell him to bug off, when I think of it. I guess I wanted to see how far he'd go. Maybe I was testing him." If Beth was testing Martin, she went to extraordinary lengths to do so. Her business allowed her to transfer from the East to the West Coast, and she did, but intrepid Martin, who traveled a great deal in his own business, showed up in L.A. along with her! He began flying in on a regular basis and taking her out to dinner — which Beth, reluctantly, allowed herself to do with him. "I'd never met anyone like Martin. He scared me a little. I mean, he had to be neurotic to keep after me like this, didn't he? It never occurred to me he might actually love me. I guess I so deeply didn't like myself that his truly caring for me seemed out of the question." Beth realizes now that she'd spent much of her early life, starting with her father and continuing with two bad marriages, bending over backward to please men but never getting any sense of being loved in return. Her father was always distant, and neither of her husbands really gave her the spontaneous love and affection she craved. She'd set her hopes on at least having children, but then she developed a health condition that required her hysterectomy. "It was as if God were telling me I'd failed. I couldn't have or do anything like normal women. After spending so much of my life trying to get men to give me happiness, I finally broke down. It simply would never work."

But now there is Martin. "He keeps telling me how

much he likes me — for me. Now that I'm in therapy, I'm sort of using my therapist as a reality checker, to get her opinion of whether Martin really loves me or not. What I'm learning is that I am lovable, even though I'm fat and I can't have kids. Even after having gone through so many disappointing relationships, I'm learning that maybe it's okay to take another chance, so I'm giving Martin a chance. I'm trying not to push him away. It's hard. My natural instinct is to start arguments or create distance or to find something wrong. But there Martin is again, popping up like a cork in the ocean, telling me it's okay, I can trust him, I don't have to be afraid."

Beth may decide eventually that Martin isn't for her. But her immediate task is to accept herself as likable — something Gloria hasn't been able to do. Once she makes that leap to accepting and loving herself, she'll be able to make more realistic decisions about getting a man into her life. Again, she has to pay attention to *who she is* before she can expand her life to include others. And those others, as I've suggested elsewhere in this book, don't always have to be men, either. Women friends can fill much of our need for companionship and closeness.

This brings us to a crucial question: What do we mean when we say we "need" a man?

■■■■■■■■■■■■■■■

Defining Your Need for a Man

If you want a man in your life, the most important question you can ask yourself is, "Why do I want him?" Not necessarily to talk yourself *out* of that want, but to clarify what it is you're really after. Do you want to be taken care of? Do you want someone to share your interests and feelings with? Do you want the financial security of marrying someone with money? Are you on the rebound from a painful breakup, and do you feel the need to drown yourself in a new relationship, quickly? Perhaps you want someone for status, or as a companion. Or maybe you just want a man because everyone else you know "has" one. Sometimes we use men to medicate ourselves, not unlike the way people drink or take sedatives to avoid facing reality. Do you reflexively turn to men to keep from looking at yourself?

It's perfectly natural for a woman to want to be with a man; a "friends and lovers" relationship is one of the most wonderful things that you can have. But you do need to define your needs as clearly as you can to be sure you're not kidding yourself. You can't turn to a man, just as you can't turn to any other outside source, as a panacea for all your woes. All a man is, is a man, a human being with peculiarities and special interests and flaws and potential, just like you. We get into trouble when we start to mythologize men, when we see men as representative of some fantasy or simplistic assumption. When, inevitably, the man doesn't live up to our unrealistic expectations, we're devastated or we see it as evidence of what we've always "known": men are impossible; we'll never find love; we might as well give up.

When Penny married Ron, she saw him as perfect. In a lucrative, long-established business with his father, he was doing well and she was assured of financial security. She liked his parents, and she treated them respectfully. Her own home life had been unhappy, and she was used to taking her problems to Ron, even before they married. He listened and he cared, and he almost always came up with a solution. So it was no surprise that when they got married, Penny willingly turned her life over to him. He'd already demonstrated his ability to take care of her.

Ron's family became hers; her income became his. He preferred his friends to hers, and she went along with him, ceasing to see most of the people she'd known before. It was only when she became pregnant almost two years after they got married that she began to feel that her life might not be so perfect after all. At the news of her imminent grandchild, Ron's mother all but moved into their home, watching over Penny like a hawk, directing her diet, decorating the baby's room — taking over. "That's my grandchild you've got in your oven," she joked, "and we want him well done!" The key to their house they'd given to Ron's parents for emergencies was now used almost every day; Ron's mother and dad let themselves into the apartment whenever they liked. "Just checking," they'd explain, as they walked in at eight in the morning or right before lunch or dinner. "We just wanted to see if you needed anything . . . if you'd brought up your mail . . . if you left the light on. . . ."

Penny thought she was going crazy. She complained to Ron about his parents' constant meddling, but Ron just didn't have the heart to tell his mother and father to cool it. He tried to smooth things over by telling Penny they'd let up once the baby was born — this was their first grandchild, after all, and of course they'd be concerned and excited. But he couldn't placate Penny entirely. She hated being treated like a child, which was exactly how her in-laws seemed to see her. She also began to realize something about her husband. Ron was a sweet boy, but although he now had a wife and would soon have a baby, he hadn't become a man, in his own eyes or his parents'.

Penny thought she had married someone who would be her friend, lover, protector, provider, and savior. And yet Ron absented himself from the growing conflict between Penny and his parents; he was allowing her to take the full brunt of it. She felt guilty about complaining: Ron's parents had helped them out financially; they were helping to provide their son and daughter-in-law with the very food they ate. She felt, sometimes, that she was the one at fault, that she was failing. She knew that her in-laws couldn't understand it when she expressed resentment at their constant presence and suggestions: she had taken their son and their money; the least she could do was take them, too.

But she couldn't take them: she finally had a blowup with both Ron and his parents. She said she could no longer stand their meddling, and she couldn't understand why Ron was never really on her side. What kind of husband was he, anyway? And should she stay with him? Angry and hurt, they all said things they later regretted. Penny didn't know where to turn, or to whom. She'd cut all her previous ties; now she tried to resuscitate them. She called her stepmother and asked if she could spend some time with her. Her stepmother's response was succinct and typically cold: "You made your bed, now lie in it." Penny felt completely abandoned. She broke down in front of Ron. But Ron finally came through. He held her in his arms, comforted her, and then made his own confession: standing up to his parents was the most difficult thing for him to do, but he knew now, for both their sakes, that he'd have to. He decided to quit the family business and get another job, but this would mean Penny would have to go back to work after the baby was born.

Penny suddenly realized that the financial security Ron and his family had always represented wasn't important anymore. She willingly agreed to Ron's plan. She felt closer to Ron than she ever had. Here, finally, was the man she'd sought. He had grown up, in her eyes and in his own. This marked a new beginning for them both: there was some sacrifice and pain in this new beginning, and some strained family relationships for a while, but they had wrested their lives back. They were no longer attached to Ron's parents' apron strings. Now Penny decided she wanted a man for himself and not for the wrappings he came in — the family and connections and money. And in facing and accepting Ron for who he really was, she was learning to face and accept herself. But, most important, Penny had allowed *herself* to grow up. In facing who Ron really was, she was also facing that her decision to be with him was her own: she was accepting responsibility for her role in their relationship in a way crucial to the sense of self-reliance we've been talking about throughout this book.

What I've found — and what women I know who've developed happy lives have found — is that the more you pour into what you can do for yourself, focusing on your own capacities and interests and potential, the more you make yourself receptive to good relationships. Penny's mistake was in thinking she could find happiness by subsuming herself in Ron and his family and the privileges they provided. When, as Penny did, you pour your energy into pursuing someone, and that pursuit becomes the fuel of the relationship, you'd better be prepared to keep pursuing once you've gotten into that relationship. Ron and his parents were responding to Penny in the way they did because Penny had given them the clear message, from the start, that she thought they were more important than she was. So of course it was all right to take her life over — she'd handed it to them! They were only doing what she'd invited them to do. Growing up for Penny meant, as we've seen, learning to take her life back where it belongs: in her own safekeeping.

Sometimes, despite all your efforts, love *doesn't* come. Sometimes it's neither a dividend nor the product of a meticulous search. And because love won't always come on cue or simply because you want it to come, it becomes even more crucial to learn to be satisfied with yourself on your own. However, this said, if having a man in your life is critical at this time, here *are* some practical tips you might keep in mind to increase your chances of meeting the man *you* want to meet. They work best in the context we've already described: the context of paying attention to *you* so that you radiate more self-confidence and self-love.

■ ■ ■ ■ ■ ■ ■ ■ ■ ■ ■ ■ ■ ■

The Self-Reliant Woman's Guide to Meeting a Man

Many women, like Gloria, don't believe they can have a social life as single women: they instantly equate the term *social life* with couples or with very young singles. However, you can create your own social life, and it doesn't have to take place in a bar or at a dance or a late-night party. Cultivate friendships. Invite a small group of people to dinner; meet new people by having two friends bring two people you don't know. Enjoy each other as potential friends, not potential "conquests." See whose interests match whose. Let networks happen naturally. When you meet a woman who you think would enjoy meeting an acquaintance of yours because of shared interests, make the introductions. Reach out, be available, and you'll discover the favor will be returned — usually much more abundantly then you anticipated.

Equally essential is to have a clear idea of who — and what kind of relationship — you're looking for. I have compiled a description that, when I share it with women at lectures, always seems to elicit requests for copies. This gave me the idea to suggest writing the description on a 3 × 5 card to carry with you, to remind yourself not only of the kind of relationship you're after, but of the kind of person you want to be in that relationship. Here it is:

I am looking for someone:

Who is happy with himself;

Who is seeking to enhance his life with the presence of another whom he is not interested in changing or restricting;

Who will be happy for my success and support me in my failures;

Who will be neither overprotective nor indifferent, and should we leave each other, will allow it to be a sweet ending, one in which each of us will try to leave the other at least as well off as we were before we met, acknowledging that we are better off as a result of experiencing each other.

Write this, if you like, on your own 3 × 5 card and keep it as a reminder of the kind of relationship that you're really after. Let it act as a guideline when you do meet a man: will he give you the kind of respect and attention you deserve, the true caring implicit in this description?

Meeting candidates for that wonderful relationship *is* the obvious problem, however. You've heard all the tips about going to art galleries, libraries, operas and concerts, even Laundromats rather than singles bars to meet men, and perhaps you've tried those avenues but with no success. If you haven't been successful, it may be because you're putting too much pressure on yourself to connect. When you let up on yourself, surprising things can happen. One woman told me she occasionally met men at cemeteries! When she visited her mother's grave, she'd sometimes meet men who were also visiting loved ones' graves. "My mother was always trying to get me to meet men," she smiles. "Who realized she'd go to these lengths?"

The problem is, when you go to an art gallery to meet a man without having any genuine interest in the art, you've put yourself in a doubly awkward situation: you're there with an emotionally high-charged agenda doing something you'd never do out of your own interest. Don't go to places that don't already interest you! It seems a simple suggestion, but if you go to a concert because you're really interested in the music, you'll have an extra enthusiasm to bring to the venture — an enthusiasm that will make itself felt by any others you may meet and that will make your evening enjoyable whether you meet anyone or not. When you indulge in something interesting or pleasurable to you, you radiate something to other people and thus increase your chances of meeting someone whose interests and temperament you might truly share. And if you don't, what's the loss? You'll still have done something you enjoy, something to enrich yourself.

So choose meeting places first on the basis of how much they already interest you, and only secondarily for the relationships they might spontaneously make possible.

Similarly, do anything you can do to increase your self-esteem. Do things that make you like yourself. Sometimes this can be cosmetic: don't you feel terrific when you know you've got a great haircut? Don't you feel wonderful when you know a certain dress sets you off to great advantage? Take pleasure in these things because they make you feel good. You can't help radiating your best self when you pay this kind of attention to yourself. It may sound like an odd tip for meeting a man, but one of the best pieces of advice I can give you is to learn to have fun!

Many women, asked if they do anything to enjoy themselves — something they love, that they do for the pure pleasure of it — look at you blankly. "For me?" is the general, surprised response. "Well, no, not exactly. I mean, after my job, after I've finished with the kids . . . I guess I enjoyed that vacation I took three years ago, but . . ." Do you do anything for fun — sheer, unadulterated fun? I can't tell you the effect of giving yourself carteblanche permission to enjoy yourself. If that enjoyment takes you out into the park to fly a kite or out to the pier to see the sunset or into the mountains to breathe fresh air; or to three double features in two days or an ice cream parlor to have (just this once!) a hot fudge sundae or a wine-tasting or gourmet-food shopping expedition; if it takes you to a natural-history museum to see the dinosaurs you loved as a kid or to a fashionable jewelry or clothing store to (at the very least) window-shop — whatever fun means to you, indulge yourself occasionally! I can't stress enough how much this will open you to the world and, not incidentally, to the people you'll inevitably bump into. This is how you meet people — not by poring over some "How to Catch a Man" makeup or clothing guide, not by squeezing yourself into uncomfortable situations you think are your only alternatives. Remember, if you can't enjoy your own company, why would you think someone else will?

Do you see how our principles of self-reliance and self-growth can aid you even through the inevitable trials of love? What I hope this chapter and the preceding one have made clear is that whatever your love agenda — whether it's finding a man, deciding to leave a man, or even deciding that you don't for the moment particularly *want* a man in your life — you have the resources to protect yourself and direct yourself to options that serve *you*. "Reasonable love" isn't the contradiction you may think it is: you can bring the same careful consideration for yourself to love that you bring to every other area of your life. Sometimes old feelings of fear and vulnerability get activated when things don't work out, but the work you've done in the first chapters of this book, as well as the consideration you're now giving yourself by contemplating love in some new ways, will help you develop all the resources you need to hold on until those frightening feelings pass — which they will.

Let's now focus our consideration on a still wider arena: who we are, and who we can become, in our work lives. It's time to take your new self-reliance to your job. Prepare for some surprising rewards!

8

....

Making Your Work Work for You

....

STUDIES show that 68 percent of women with children under eighteen are in the work force, and women who work full-time still earn only sixty-six cents to a man's dollar. Simple statistics reveal what most of us already know: more women are working than ever before, and yet women still earn less than men do. Some of the disparity in men's and women's salaries can be attributed to the fact that so many women work in low-paying "pink collar" jobs, either because they aren't trained for anything else or because those jobs may appear more suited to child-rearing (the hours are clear-cut so that a working mother can depend on getting home when she has to, for example). But the disparity also reflects the fact that women still haven't, to any great degree, penetrated the higher levels of corporate power. Among Fortune 500 companies, less than 2 percent of top executives are women. Women who do succeed to top executive posts earn 42 percent less than their male counterparts. Although during the past two decades feminists have made injustices like these no secret, and while things *have* gotten better than they were twenty and thirty years ago (largely as a result of these same feminists' call to arms), it's clear that women are still getting the short end of the job-market stick. However, you don't have to be one of those women.

We've already seen how cultural assumptions about women have held us back; statistics make it clear that they continue to hold us back in the work force. While the bad news is that cultural assumptions change slowly, the good news is that, as individual women, we do not have to match that snail's pace. I'd like to suggest that, by applying the message of this book, the exercises I've shown you, and the perspective you've been developing, you can start to make a difference in your own work experience — right now. You have the power to define and reinvent yourself at work just as much as you do in the rest of your life. You can beat the odds suggested by the statistics I've just cited by practicing the same principles of self-definition and self-reliance on the job that you're learning to practice in your relationships and self-view.

But first, we need to acknowledge something more than just that we've got the *power* to reinvent ourselves across the board — we need to reaffirm our *right* to reinvent ourselves. Like many women, you may have been so entrenched in the Feminine Mistake of relying on the outside world to tell you what to do that you're still secretly uncomfortable with the suggestion that you could (or even should) start relying on yourself. It's hard to develop the self-esteem to call the shots in your own life when you've grown up believing that you don't truly *have* a self all your own. Progress toward the kind of self-reliance I'd like you to achieve is sometimes slow: it takes time to prove to yourself that you've got all the resources you need within you to make a life — or improve your job situation. And nowhere do our doubts about our power to change things seem to loom larger than in the workplace.

In fact, probably the hardest test of self-reliance that women face comes when they walk through the office door. As deserving as we may know we are, the reality most of us face at work can sometimes throw us back into our worst doubts and fears. Even young women in their early twenties, just now graduating from college and entering the job market — women who did not grow up with the implicit message that men were more "competent" than women — slam into a work reality that teaches them that men are still the leaders. For proof, take a look again at the statistics with which we began this chapter.

What real control do we have over our work lives? Is the answer to try to overcompensate, to give 120 percent, just as we've done in our relationships? As you've already seen and heard (and may have experienced firsthand), this notion of Superwoman just didn't work: it left too many of us exhausted and burned out. Women who try to have it all often realize that they've been just as hoodwinked by the promise that they can, as any 1950s housewife was by the promise that she would find perfect fulfillment in the kitchen. Again, when the directive comes from outside ourselves, we're misdirected.

But what work goals *is* it reasonable to have?

Answering that question doesn't only require some understanding of the cultural blocks that women face at work; you also need to examine the prejudices that you personally may have about work — kneejerk reactions you may not even be aware of but that are needlessly holding you back. One enormous set of prejudices, for example, has accumulated around something we hear hotly debated again and again: the Mommy Track. Let's try to clear away some of the steam that surrounds this term to see what's really at issue.

■■■■■■■■■■■■■■

To Mommy Track — or Not

When Felice Schwartz's now-famous article about what has come to be called the Mommy Track (a term Felice Schwartz did not herself use in the article) appeared in the January/February 1989 *Harvard Business Review*, she was attacked with astonishing vituperativeness by some women. The premise of Felice Schwartz's article that was attacked was simply that if a woman were to decide to work *and* have a family, it would be a reasonable and humane alternative for both employer and employee to agree to certain adjustments, allowing the working mother a less demanding work track that would enable her to deal more effectively with both her job and raising children. In other words, she could take the "local" rather than the "express" route in her career for a while if she chose to do so. Some women denounced this as an invitation to (usually male) employers to hold women back: no woman on the Mommy Track, they said, ever has a realistic chance of advancing in her career, even if the woman decides, after her children are grown, to get off the Mommy Track and back on the "express." It was a regressive idea, said those who were outraged, and would simply give men more reason to keep women from competing with them.

The very term Mommy Track has become so negative that few women would dare to admit that they might actually want to do what it suggested. And yet, what does the term really mean? Is prejudice against a term that has acquired pejorative connotations clouding our ability to assess what Felice Schwartz was really proposing?

Long before the term was coined, many women were following a Mommy Track — choosing jobs whose hours and responsibilities would permit them to take adequate care of their children. I was one of these women: when my children were young, I took a job as a school psychologist whose hours, 8:45 to 4:00, enabled me to get home in time to be with my family. It was a good job for my circumstances, even though it did not give me as much freedom and creative opportunity as I would later seek from work. But that's the point: like thousands of women, I was eventually able to build from what would now be called a Mommy Track job toward a satisfying career when, after my children were older, I could devote more time to that career. This relates crucially to the message of this book: if you have the desire and the ability and the self-belief, you can turn whatever circumstances you're in to better advantage, including Mommy Tracking. I know numerous women who've Mommy Tracked in this way — an interior decorator, a real estate saleswoman, a commercial artist among them — all of whom are now exceedingly successful in their careers.

It's not that there aren't exploitive employers (men *and* women) who may turn a Mommy Tracker's slower pace to their own advantage. However, not every woman *wants* to become a CEO, and, from a practical point of view, ensuring that a woman keeps a job she needs, even if it remains at a middle-management level, need not have a negative connotation, as long as the woman herself is content. If she's not, then she has more resources to move ahead than she may realize, even in the face of an oppressive employer.

That's part of what this chapter will help you to explore: the ways you can reconstruct your working life, no

matter what the negative circumstances you have to con-
tend with, so that you end up doing what you really want.
Maybe all you want is to pay the rent. Maybe you're after
creative freedom. Maybe you want the power of being a
CEO. Whatever it is, and whether or not you've decided
to Mommy Track during any part of your life, your goals
are far more achievable than you may think.

Let's take a look at some of those negative circumstances, some of the blocks that seem to be holding you
back from getting what you want at work. You'll discover
that you have a lot more power over these blocks than
you think, and that you may be shortchanging yourself
in ways you never realized. Witness the following story
about a woman who thought she was following her own
path, but discovered she was really following somebody
else's — her husband's. How she woke up to her ability
to change an oppressive working situation has resonance
for all of us, whether married or single, as you'll see.

■ ■ ■ ■ ■ ■ ■ ■ ■ ■ ■ ■ ■ ■

Sharing Power: Karen and Maurice

I have never seen a more exhausted-looking, bedraggled
woman than Karen the first time she came to see me.
She'd obviously made some attempt to dress up because
she knew she was going out, but her clothes and makeup
were so haphazard that it was clear to me that going out
was something she only accomplished hastily. In fact, her
first words to me were, "I hope this won't take too long —
I have to go to the dry cleaners before they close and then
home to make sure my husband's invoices get out in the
afternoon mail. . . ." Karen gave *overworked* a new meaning.

I asked her to sit down, which she allowed herself to
do — just barely. She seemed to perch on the edge of her

seat. It was clear that she wasn't used to staying anywhere for long; there was always something urgent on the horizon she had to do next. I asked her why she'd come to me, already intuiting that if seeking help from a psychologist had become urgent enough for her to take the time out of her busy day to do it, she must be very much in need of that help.

She was. "I can't take it anymore," she finally said. "I just can't keep this up." She allowed herself to sink back into the chair, took a deep breath, looked up at me and then down at her hands, which were clenched in her lap. She looked down because she had started to cry and she didn't want me to see.

"Tell me about it," I said.

"It's my husband," she started. "Maurice used to be a computer salesman for a major company, then he got the idea that he could make more money setting up his own business out of the house." Karen blew her nose and seemed to compose herself. She seemed determined to get every detail right, to give me every item of background. "At first I was thrilled. I mean, Maurice was so excited about going out on his own that I couldn't help but be happy for him. And he kept saying what a wonderful thing it would be for us to live *and* work together. From the start he assumed I'd be there to help him. Money was short at first and he couldn't afford secretarial help. But wouldn't it be wonderful to work together on a common project?" Karen managed a grim, ironic smile. "It did seem so romantic back then," she continued. "Maurice and I building our own business — I was willing to do anything he wanted me to do!"

However, what slowly became clear to Karen was that this new undertaking was not theirs as much as it was his. To drum up business, Maurice had to wine and dine clients, make business trips, do much of the field work.

That meant, of course, that Karen did all of the nitty-gritty office work (correspondence, paying bills, book-keeping, keeping track of supplies, answering the phone) back home. "I suddenly found myself doing full-time secretarial work — alone. Somehow the romantic vision I'd had was of Maurice and me working *together* as co-owners of the business, sharing responsibilities and profits equally. But that wasn't how it was working out."

Karen was, she quickly realized, expected to oversee the growing business's paperwork in addition to taking care of their two kids, who were a very active five and seven years old. "Maurice — as a favor, he kept reminding me — had put in an extra phone with a new number for the business so that phone bills would be kept apart and there would be a clear separation between where we worked and where we made personal calls." Karen drew a deep sigh. "What this ends up meaning is that I spend my time running from one room to the other every time one or the other phone rings!" Then, just a week before Karen came to see me, Johnny, their seven-year-old, broke his arm in the playground at school. "The school nurse called me with the news and I had to rush over to the school, right at the same time a client called who was only going to be in town that day and wanted to see us for a possible big deal. This was a client Maurice had been trying to get for months, an important guy . . ." Karen rubbed her temples, reliving that hectic morning. "What could I do? I had to go to Johnny — I couldn't reach Maurice." Karen says they lost that client and Maurice hit the roof.

"That's when I knew I had to get help. This great, romantic idea about having a business together had turned into a nightmare. But I can't just bail out. I just don't know what to do!" Karen said it wasn't only the work that was putting her under. "Maurice is feeling so much anxiety trying to get this business going it's had another effect I didn't anticipate. He's suddenly voracious sexually. It's like he just can't get enough!" Karen looked a little embarrassed but made herself continue. "Any number of my friends would wonder what I was complaining about," she said quietly, "but I'm aching for some *rest*. It's like there's no safe place for me to go, to be. I can't stand it anymore."

Karen was in a somewhat unusual situation — not many husbands and wives both live and work with each other — but she was operating from some very common, and damaging, assumptions. We've met these assumptions before. She felt her duties as wife meant an obligation to serve her husband in whatever ways he asked. While she says she'd had a romantic idea that their joint business venture was going to be an equal one, she didn't raise any clear objections to Maurice when it turned out to be far from equal. All she did was allow herself to get more and more miserable. What she first had to do was realize that she had the right to expect more, just as any human being who works has a right to be paid for that work.

I knew that the first thing Karen had to do was to let Maurice know that she was in an unacceptable situation. She was giving her bookkeeping, typing, and secretarial skills away for free — skills that could easily enable her to get a well-paying job outside of the house. But the second thing would be to propose a fairer plan. She had to be paid a salary. Wouldn't Maurice have to replace her with someone at great expense if she were suddenly to stop working? Wasn't she worth a weekly paycheck, too?

At first, Karen was horrified at the suggestion. "But Maurice would think I didn't love him, that I wasn't willing to sacrifice everything for this business!" I reminded Karen that loving Maurice didn't have to mean losing her identity — or working herself to an early death. If she wanted to sacrifice something in the hope that it would lead to greater benefits for both of them in the future, what about proposing that she be paid less than the going rate, at first — even as low as minimum wage — as long as it meant she could share in the company's profits to a greater degree in the future? What about asking for a percentage of the profits as well as a small weekly salary? Karen considered all this, and she decided to take the plunge that night and bring it up with Maurice. "If I had some extra money," she said, "I could hire someone to look after the kids when I'm working." It began to make real sense.

As Karen had predicted, Maurice first felt a little betrayed by the suggestion. But even he could see the untenable situation Karen had been in when she'd had to take care of Johnny and his broken arm instead of the client he'd been hoping to land. He agreed to pay her. Karen's life began to change, not only because logistically things became more manageable (she hired a high-school girl to baby-sit and help clean the house), but because her self-esteem began to rise. "I'm starting to see myself as a real working woman," she told me some weeks afterward. "I feel like my skills are worth something now. That they're not just part of the bargain my husband got when he married me." As Karen's self-esteem grew, so did what she felt were some very reasonable demands. "If I were working at a company, I'd be able to ask for a raise, maybe get into profit-sharing, even set up an IRA or Keogh account for retirement. Why should the fact that I'm working for my husband make things any different?" Karen had Maurice draw up a partnership agreement that allowed her to participate more directly in the company's profits, and she kept a separate account for her own money, skimming off 10 percent every week for savings. "It's how I pay myself," she says today.

The results of all this have gone far beyond making Karen's work life more bearable. "My home life is so much better now, too. My husband respects me more because, I guess, it's so clear that I respect myself." This even extends to sex. "I don't feel as pushed around as I did before, as if I somehow have to submit to him whenever he's in the mood. I've set some limits, and sometimes I'm the initiator in lovemaking, which rarely happened before. That equal partnership I'd dreamed about long ago now seems, with some careful work by both of us, to be coming true. And it's coming true because I'm learning to look out for myself."

Sure, things aren't quite what they'd be if she worked in another company, for a boss with whom she wasn't so intimately connected. ("Sometimes Maurice and I have a board-of-directors meeting in the bathtub," Karen says.) And she might stand to make more money elsewhere, too. But she knows her own worth now and she's choosing to trade some of the benefits she might have elsewhere for the convenience and autonomy she has in her job at home. "My life feels like my own now," Karen says. "Not like something I have to live for my husband. I can't imagine feeling any greater relief than this gives me!"

Obviously, not every woman is able to work in such close connection with her husband or lover, nor would every woman want to. But Karen's story points out something universal about waking up to your own self-worth and developing the courage to act on it. Let's look at a few other women whose circumstances are quite different from Karen's but who've learned some equally valuable lessons.

■ ■ ■ ■ ■ ■ ■ ■ ■ ■ ■ ■ ■ ■

Learning from the "Enemy": The Art of Advancement

Anna is a woman in her early forties who has, she says, learned the hard way what success is all about. "I was a dishrag when I first started working," she says. "I was fresh out of a good college, magna cum laude, and thrilled to get my first job at an advertising agency — thrilled even though the job description was 'file clerk/light secretarial.' The fact that someone wanted me for a job, that I had at least a chance to make it in the 'real world,' was heady enough. I didn't care what I did. I just wanted to get a foot in the door." Anna's foot remained, however, planted underneath her secretarial desk or next to a file cabinet. The ad agency where she worked had a firmly entrenched male hierarchy, and women very definitely, if tacitly, were expected to know their place. "Whenever I see that movie *9 to 5* I identify so much," Anna says. "Even though a lot of the real work got done by women — secretaries — the bosses, who were all men, always got the credit. I'd started working in 1972, just when feminist consciousness was beginning to have an effect, but I now see that the main effect it had on me was to turn me into a private whiner. I let my superiors treat me like a gofer; I see now that I allowed myself to be treated as a file clerk, a coffee-getter, a right-hand girl. Not that storming into any boss's office would have done anything other than get me fired, but I still didn't see the real opportunities I was missing, opportunities I might have taken advantage of earlier than I did, even at this male bastion of an agency."

Anna began to awaken to these hidden opportunities when a man named Larry arrived — a brash, young college graduate whose academic background closely resembled

Anna's but, as Anna says, who "expected to be treated like someone who was headed for the top. He had a totally different attitude than I had. I watched him, over the first few months he worked next to me, clue into how the business was run — what impressed the boss, who got the boss's ear. He was looking *analytically* at how the company ran, not emotionally. At first I thought he was arrogant. Then I realized he was smart. He saw what worked in the company, and he aped it. At that time, the head of our department was crazy about one-line ads — you know, a dramatic picture of a sunset, a gorgeous car next to the beach, and a line like, 'The good life is yours for the asking.' We used to joke that he was into heavy-drama Hallmark cards, but Larry didn't joke along with us. What he did, apart from his file-clerk duties, was spend time after hours working up ad ideas he knew would appeal to the boss, and then — charting the boss's moods carefully — ask him for some constructive criticism." Larry slowly won the boss's attention and found himself advancing up the ladder. "Okay, maybe it was partly because he was a man, but that wasn't the only reason," Anna says. "Suddenly I stopped whining about how men got the best deals and began to wonder what I could do to market my skills a little better, and in a way appropriate to the company."

Anna began to take more careful notice of how the agency operated. She realized that her lowly job as file clerk and secretary gave her access to every detail about how the company ran. She began to see the information she was paid to sort through as an opportunity, not a burden. "I began really reading the stuff I was supposed to file. I wrote up a list of questions I wanted to ask the boss — questions that wouldn't make it seem like I was nosy or pushy or trying to one-up anybody; questions I phrased so it would be apparent I was trying to understand the company better in order to do my job better." Anna began to have some ideas about streamlining production costs — ideas that occurred to her because she was paying attention to the data she now realized was passing in front of her eyes every day. "I finally decided to make an appointment with my boss to tell him some of my ideas. He was surprised, I think, that I wanted to talk to him about anything other than changing my lunch hour or vacation time, but he said, sure, he had twenty minutes that afternoon if I wanted to talk to him then. I came in prepared, not only with my ideas but with a watch. I made sure not to abuse my twenty-minute time allotment. I outlined what I thought might help streamline costs and, nineteen minutes later, said I didn't want to keep him because I knew this was all the time he had. I could tell this punctuality impressed him; I knew, anyway, that punctuality was a real thing with him. He smiled. And things began to change for me in the company."

Anna wasn't able to accomplish miracles: the company's male hierarchy remained pretty much firmly in place, even while she eventually was able to get more recognition (promotions and higher pay) than most women at that company had achieved. In fact, she now has a job at another agency that offers women more possibility for advancement: two of its vice-presidents are women. But she came with an impressive track record she was able to amass at her first job — a track record her company allowed her to develop because she had allowed them to see what she could do. "I guess what I did was give up whining about the company's injustices and replace it with a real curiosity about what it would take to turn things around."

None of this is to suggest that every job you have, get, or want is worthless unless you turn it into a stepping stone to CEO-dom. But then, not every woman wants a

high-powered corporate job. Anna illustrates something
more basic, something to add to what Karen also showed
us. When you learn to value your own skills (as Karen
did) *and* to take a practical, pragmatic view of your work
opportunities (as Anna did), you're paving your way toward fulfillment in a job. You're taking the reins of your
life into your own hands. You're applying what we've
been talking about from page one of this book to the world
out there.

There are still some obstacles women commonly face at
work that we haven't mentioned yet. Again, our conditioning is so deep-rooted that sometimes we can fall,
without wanting to or even realizing it, into roles that
sabotage our chances of succeeding or even getting along
with others at work. These negative roles aren't always
subservient: they can be highly and damagingly *compet-
itive* — especially sad when women turn against other
women on the job, out of what Luise Eichenbaum and
Susie Orbach, in their book *Between Women*, call "love,
envy and competition."

■■■■■■■■■■■■■■

Women vs. Women

Male colleagues or bosses aren't our only oppressors at
work, as you're probably all too aware. Due to what Eichenbaum and Orbach call women's merged attachments,
our expectations of each other as friends — what the au-
thors call "the easy, comfortable, and cozy feelings that
women can create together" — can make a terrible mix
with feelings of jealousy or competition that also commonly crop up at work. It seems particularly difficult for
women to set boundaries with each other: we're so conditioned to telling all to a girlfriend that we often find

ourselves revealing too much to a female colleague, saying things we'd never say to a man. And if that female colleague (from whatever motive) uses that information against us or to her own advantage, we feel peculiarly and usually devastatingly hurt. How could a friend have stabbed us in the back that way?

The reasons for this kind of backstabbing can be complicated. Eichenbaum and Orbach offer an interesting and plausible explanation: they suggest that the mother/child relationship nearly every woman experiences from infancy sets her up for conflicting expectations of women later in life, stemming from the infant daughter's conflict between merging with the mother and breaking free and becoming independent. My own clinical experience supports this: a crucial task for almost every woman I've worked with has been to reconcile "I love you" with "I need to go my own way." This doesn't come near to revealing the whole story about the roots of women's relationships with each other, but it at least hints at the reasons for some of the ambivalence most women feel today when they find themselves working together.

Added to this is the cultural conditioning to compete for male attention, which simply reinforces women's separateness from one another. The hard truth is that women do often continue to fight each other for a man — or, by extension, for approval from an authority, which in business is, more often than not, male. Unfortunately, that fight for male or authoritative approbation can be terribly destructive: more than one friendship between women has been wiped out because of it. We can be hypercritical of each other in very personal ways that may have nothing to do with the job or our degree of competence: tearing down each other's looks, age, weight, makeup, clothes, judging each other as harshly as we secretly fear others are judging us. This is especially sad because this hypercritical judgment isn't often something we're consciously *choosing* to make: we're defensive out of reflex, out of the deep conditioning I've just talked about. And so we hurt each other without really wanting to — or needing to.

What does all this have to do with our theme of learning to define yourself and then relying on that self-definition?

A great deal. When you react to conditioning, conditioning that makes you do what you truly don't want to do, you're relying on reflex, and reacting reflexively is a kind of bondage. You don't have the control over your behavior that conscious reflection can give you, which means you can't direct your own life out of free choice. Any definition you come up with for your life therefore isn't entirely your own: part of it is simply unthinking adherence to conditioning. This reliance on reflex can blind you to so much of what your behavior is really about.

You may, for example, relate to this topic of women vs. women from the standpoint of victim, remembering all the times in your life you felt or said, "How could she have done this to me?"; but if you look into yourself deeply enough, you will probably find evidence that you've done a little betraying yourself. You may never have meant to betray someone, and you may have hidden the fact that it *was* a betrayal by rationalizing it with thoughts like, "Well, if *she* hadn't done what she did, *I* wouldn't have retaliated. . . ." But the truth is that, reflexively, you probably have at one time or another lashed out defensively. When we mercilessly compete, judge each other, feel jealous, or otherwise behave without thinking, we're not living freely out of choice. It's pretty much an axiom that the extent to which our lives are based on free choice is the extent to which we can find happiness. That's why this issue is so important to explore — so that we can gain some conscious control over one more area of negative conditioning, one more area that stands in the way of not only success in our jobs but something perhaps more precious: our friendships with each other.

■■■■■■■■■■■■■■

Women, Friendship, and Work

Two women I met recently can help us explore this issue. They offer an instructive — and inspiring — tale about how they've managed to overcome some of these deeply bred competition and judgment difficulties.

Monia Joblin, Vice-President of Original Programming at USA Network, and Bonnie Hammer, who not long ago became Director of Original Programming at USA Network, had a kind of "Kate and Allie" relationship: they shared an apartment when they were getting started in their careers and became very close friends. They offered each other moral support as well as whatever career leads each came upon. When Monia got her job at USA Network, she got an intriguing idea. She was now responsible for hiring a Director of Original Programming, and she quite simply couldn't imagine anyone better suited for the job — anyone more competent, talented, creative, or responsible — than Bonnie!

Over dinner and wine with Bonnie, Monia broached the possibility of Bonnie working for her. Bonnie was intrigued, but wary. "What if I screw up?" she asked Monia. "Will you treat me like any other employee?" Bonnie wondered how she would feel about taking orders from her best friend — could friendship and career mix? As much as she wanted Bonnie to take the position, Monia also had some doubts. They were in a business where people were almost expected to jump around from job to job — what if Bonnie decided to leave after Monia had grown to depend on her? Could their friendship survive that?

But as many doubts as the two friends had about mixing business with friendship, they still wanted to try. The prospect of working with each other was appealing not only because they liked and trusted each other so much, but because Bonnie really was so suited for the position Monia wanted her to take, and it was exactly the kind of job Bonnie was looking for. So they took the plunge, and they've made some interesting discoveries.

The first big lesson working with each other taught them was the importance of making a clear separation between issues and personality. Bonnie says, "We've learned to set boundaries. We steer away from talking about personal problems once we've walked into the office — as much as we'll gladly talk about them once we're *out* of the office. When we argue at work — which, heaven knows, we do! — we make it clear that we're arguing about issues, not what personal or psychological motives might be making us take one stand or another." However, Bonnie says that she's certainly aware of Monia's emotional state, and she takes it into account in their working life. "When Monia's in a bad mood — and I can pick up on her moods faster than anyone else — sometimes I'll stick my head through her office doorway and say, 'Don't make a decision about this now; you're in a bad mood!' I mean, it's not like we don't have a sense of humor about things, and we can't pretend we don't know each other as well as we do. But we can still keep from overstepping bounds."

Monia recalls her first job, which gave her some warnings about what *not* to do when working with a woman who is also a friend. "My first boss, a woman, set up dynamics that made me react to her as if she were my mother, a mother I felt I had to second-guess and sort of

therapeutically nurture. The emotional load of our working relationship became too heavy; I kept playing the
daughter who had to take care of her mother, feeling I
had to prove my worth and loyalty to her every moment.
Work became a kind of therapy; our emotional demands
got hopelessly mixed up with what we were supposed to
be accomplishing on the job. It was a mess. And when I
got out of that job, I vowed never to let a working relationship turn into that kind of mess again."

Monia has also been in situations where she's witnessed women playing roles that were a lot less nurturing.
"Women often give lip-service to the camaraderie they
feel with other women," Monia said, "but I can't tell you
the number of times I've seen women betray their female
colleagues — either by taking credit for something another woman really did, or by playing a game of one-
upmanship, 'telling on her' to the boss." As a result of
her experiences, Monia has learned to look for certain
traits in women she hires. In fact, many female executives
now do. Sydelle Albert, a freelance producer, has made a
list of them, along with their opposites. Here they are:

Toxic Traits	*Nurturing Traits*
Playing up to power	Ambition that doesn't compromise integrity
Using intimidation and bullying tactics	Secure within herself; doesn't need to throw her weight around
Isolated, and oversecretive; out only for her own gain	A team player
Jealous of other women's talents or competence	Recognizes and appreciates other women's talents and competence

Feels, "There's only room for me"	Feels, "There's always room for others"
Thinks, "Nice gals don't win"	Thinks, "Nice gals deserve to win — and they can"

These traits imply an important general truth: when you feel secure within yourself, when you learn to value your talents and potential and accept that you have abundant resources to deal with life, in or out of the office, almost organically you'll find that you'll ease up in your dealings with others, particularly other women. The attitude of self-reliance we've been developing throughout this book is a spacious and embracing one: it always allows room for other people. Life isn't a paranoid game of one-upmanship, of making sure you've got your share at all costs.

Not that there's anything wrong with ambition: being ambitious in the healthiest sense means wanting abundance for yourself and believing you have a right to it. You do have that right, and you're learning in these pages how to exercise it. But when ambition becomes clenched — when you start to lose the trust in yourself that tells you that you've got all the resources you need to deal with whatever life puts on your plate — you move away from the possibility of happiness. Those toxic traits rarely develop because we choose them; they usually come out of fear and insecurity — the fear that if you don't take measures to one-up everyone else, you'll be trampled on. Looking out for yourself is essential, as we've seen, but looking out for yourself at the expense of compassion and integrity becomes a clear route to misery. You can't be happy if you spend your life looking over your shoulder.

Out of all the experience I've had as a woman who works — and the experience of thousands of women with whom I've spoken and from whom I've learned — I've found several universal tips that can help to ensure you stay on a healthy course at work; tips that will allow you to achieve your work ambitions without needlessly hurting others; tips that will allow you to be at peace with who you are and what you want out of work. Let's take a look at them now.

■■■■■■■■■■■■■■

The Healthy Woman's Guide to Happiness on the Job: Five Tips

1. Separate business from friendship.

This follows from what Monia and Bonnie learned from working with each other: the need to set clear boundaries between personal life and what goes on at work. It's important to remember that you're at work to do a job, not to play out what's going on in your life outside the job.

2. Be careful whom you tell it all to.

As we've seen, women are prone (as a result of conditioning) to confuse expressing themselves honestly on the job with confession, especially in working relationships with other women. You don't have to reveal everything you think or feel; you don't have to let everyone know what you think about other people at work, too. Don't open yourself up to exploitation; avoid gossip. Which leads us to our next tip:

3. Learn when to be a passive listener.

Working in the "real world" means there will always be times when you'll find yourself privy to inside information about others at work — times when you can't avoid listening to gossip. If you can't escape the conversation, just listen — don't feel you have to contribute. Gossip at work is dangerous, and basing decisions on hearsay can get everyone into trouble. Listen if you have to, but reserve judgment on what you hear. And keep silent yourself.

4. Focus on what you have to do rather than whom you have to do it with.

Inevitably at work there will be people with whom you won't click. But you don't have to let that lack of chemistry get in the way of your common goal — to get the project done. Remember our "Think aikido" principle from our emotional fitness exercises? Let negative energy go by; don't latch onto it or allow yourself to get into arguments that have more to do with affect than effect. Focus on the work you're there to accomplish; you'll make it easier all around if you do.

5. When you need to ask for personal time, keep it simple.

Sometimes your personal life does intrude into work time — a child, husband, or friend may suddenly take ill and need you; you may have a doctor's appointment that can be scheduled only during the working day; you may have to rush home because your neighbor just called you about a flood in the basement. When these kinds of emergencies come up, you don't need to tell your boss or colleagues every detail; keep it as brief and simple as possible. Don't say, for example, "I have to go to the doctor for a Pap smear"; say, "I have a doctor's appointment I couldn't schedule any other time." Be as businesslike as you can about the intrusions of your personal life: don't let emergencies become an excuse to "confess all." You'll be respected more, and you'll protect yourself from saying things that, on calmer reflection, you realize you'd rather not have everyone know.

These Five Tips sum up an overarching message, one that I hope you'll take to heart whenever you leave for work. You have the opportunity to be yourself in a very special way in your work life: you get to learn about, and demonstrate, your competence as a woman who can contribute to the world. The self-esteem that organically results will do more than you dream to help you get the fulfilled life you're after. Because this self-esteem is so precious, you need to take steps to protect it, to make sure you don't make yourself needlessly vulnerable. What these tips are meant to do is to make it clear that setting the right boundaries at work doesn't limit your options, but rather gives you the real opportunity to expand them, to be all you can be as a productive woman. Of the many dividends of developing and sustaining self-esteem at work — increased self-respect, respect from others, a feeling of competence in your skills, security in becoming self-supporting — perhaps the most welcome is the simplest, and the one you probably opened this book most in the hope of finding: fulfillment. Now that you've got some clear ideas about how to earn that dividend, why not go out and acquire it?

9

....

Don't Make a Wish, Make a Life

....

Do you remember the old "Dick and Jane" books, the ones used in the public schools to teach young children to read? What I remember most about them is the longing they stirred in me. The impish brother and sister, their cheerful, neatly groomed, loving mother, and their strong, good-natured father who was always there for them lived happily in a snug, spic-and-span house. There was even a wonderful, white-haired granny who baked cookies. That's what it's like for other kids, I used to think to myself. Only my life is different.

Lucky for me, I met someone — someone I didn't tell you about when I gave you my childhood story at the beginning of this book. She was Leah: a vibrant, intelligent, successful woman, later to become my mother-in-law; a woman who helped me realize that the unhappy circumstances in which I grew up needn't stand in the way of my future growth and happiness. The fact that my mother was a fearful, bitter woman who never seemed to know pleasure or even simple satisfaction didn't necessarily condemn me to a joyless existence. The fact that my father disappeared when I was still a toddler didn't mean that I was unlovable. The fact that I didn't think I was considered particularly smart, pretty, or talented didn't mean I was doomed to a life of failure.

Leah taught me, more by example than by anything she said, that it was possible to re-create one's life. But wishing wasn't enough, and it wouldn't happen overnight. It was a matter of defining goals and then moving toward them step-by-step, taking advantage of opportunities when none were offered.

She taught me something else: even if the shiny brass ring proved elusive, the efforts expended in reaching for it were never wasted. The challenge itself could enrich my life by expanding my range of experience. More important, the frustration and disappointment of meeting failure head-on could make me stronger. Not better, necessarily, but more resilient, more confident, less fearful of falling flat on my face the next time around, because I'd already been there!

Leah didn't know it, but she taught me how to start from exactly where I was and, with practically nothing but my own resources, to build a better life for myself.

Every day I hear from women who grew up, as I did, feeling the pain of being excluded when the good things in life — material advantages, the support and encouragement of loving parents — were passed around, and who feel that nothing they can do now will make up for their early deprivation. Women who are convinced that past mistakes or present circumstances condemn them to a bleak future. Women who feel hopelessly mired in a bad marriage, a dead-end relationship, a nothing job, or who are afraid it's too late for love or achievement. Women who want to change but think they can't.

But the truth is, every single one of us has almost un-
limited opportunities to grow in ways that will bring more
love and happiness into our lives. We've spent this book
exploring some of the ways in which you can allow yourself to discover in yourself not only the potential to be
something better, but the resources to bring that potential
to fruition, and the strength to sustain the changes you
make. What you've discovered is that you can rely on
yourself to a degree you may have never before thought
possible.

Trusting in that self-reliance does, as we've seen, take
courage and a willingness to challenge ourselves and take
the first small steps away from the past and into a better
future. I know. It's scary. Uncharted territory always is.
But maybe you had a great-grandmother who helped settle
the West, or who came here from another country, not
knowing the language or the customs, but who managed
to forge a new life for herself anyway. You have some of
that courage. It's there, though perhaps you haven't
reached inside, pulled it out, and used it lately.

It's time to use it now. The alternative is to become
resigned to the way things are. We all know someone who
has acted out the charade of a loveless marriage for five,
ten, twenty years without trying to figure out how to
improve her situation, either by working toward a better
relationship with her husband or by planning ahead to
ensure future survival on her own. We all know someone
who is divorced or who has never married and, instead of
attempting to enrich herself emotionally, intellectually,
and professionally as a single woman, has put her entire
life on hold, simply waiting it out until she could be part
of a couple. Or someone who toils away in an office behind a counter somewhere, unhappy, underpaid, and functioning far below her potential, but who has nevertheless
neglected to upgrade her skills, take a course, or even

investigate other job options. Isn't it amazing that we can learn to be so comfortable with our pain?

The comfort of what is — even when what is makes us miserable — can be immobilizing. That's why it's so important to challenge ourselves. But just as it's foolhardy to try to run a marathon if you haven't trained for it, making sweeping changes in your life before you are ready for them can have disastrous repercussions. Acting impulsively or irresponsibly, bailing out of commitments, rashly leaving a husband or lover or job, or rushing headlong into a new relationship or situation before you have prepared yourself by growing and becoming stronger is practically a prescription for disaster.

Unfortunately, we live in an age of instant coffee and microwave ovens that cook dinner in a fraction of the time it took our mothers to put food on the table. We turn on the radio or TV to hear talk-show psychologists suggest that they can solve all of our problems in five minutes. We're primed for quick fixes. It seems to me that this short-cut ethic has gotten many of us into trouble. It contributes to the belief that every endeavor should be easy and effortless and yield immediate results. It encourages us to leap before we look, never mind that we're unprepared for the emotional and financial consequences.

We need to steer a course down the middle. We can get unstuck from the past, take control, and re-create ourselves and our relationships, and we can do all these things without upsetting the applecart of our existence. How? Again, by learning to trust ourselves as our own best guides. By nurturing the belief in, and practice of, self-reliance. I said at the outset that this is a book about making choices. Now you realize it's also a book about believing that you have the ability to make choices.

■■■■■■■■■■■■■■

A Recap

Take a moment to remind yourself of what you've learned about that ability; take a moment to see yourself in the light of the "clear day" I hope we've made possible. What have you learned in this book, and exactly how useful is it?

First of all, remember where we started: confronting the Feminine Mistake. Now that you see how this pervasive, damaging assumption that happiness and direction can be found only outside yourself has beleaguered other women's lives, can you see how it's gotten in your way, too? Think back to the revised life story you created for yourself: remember the ways you've learned to look at yourself from a different perspective, not with the motivation of blaming anyone or anything for your difficulties, but to take stock so that you can see what really has made you who you are — to see your strengths and weaknesses so that you can appreciate the resources you're working with.

Now think back to the Facts of Life. Do they have a new resonance for you now? Take the time to review them, one by one:

- No one can bring your life to you.
- No matter what you do in life, someone important to you isn't going to like it.
- Though it's painful, rejection won't kill you — and it may even lead to growth.
- Every choice means giving up something else.
- Some people are not capable of giving you what you're trying to get from them.
- The way you treat yourself sets the standard for others.

- There are no quick fixes that can permanently change your life.
- Life is on a rheostat, not an on/off switch.
- Some problems cannot be solved, but you can make peace with them.

What do these Facts of Life add up to now? Do you see that from first to last they invite you to take the reins of your own life? To accept responsibility for your life because no one else can do that for you? Remember that these facts aren't there to chastise you or limit you: they're there to bring clarity. They're there to give you some ground rules about how to go after — and how not to go after — the happiness you are after.

Think back to the concrete ways we've learned to begin living from the perspective that these facts of life engender. Think back to how poor, victimized Claire, debilitated by excruciating headaches, learned that the only person who was truly victimizing her was herself. Remember how she enabled herself to rethink and replan her life, step-by-step, via the Four Rs — recognition, realization, reassessment, and re-creation — and how you've explored making them part of your own life, too. Have you started to keep a journal? Remember what an invaluable tool of self-exploration and self-assessment it can be: how it can help you keep track of your progress through the Four Rs and appreciate the strides you'll inevitably make.

Don't forget the sustenance of our emotional fitness exercises — how they can help you to keep on track once you've begun to make positive change in your life. *Be with yourself:* give yourself time, whether during a walk or in meditation, to learn to identify your own voice, separate it from the hypercritical, disapproving other voices that may have directed you and held you back.

Think aikido: remember that you don't have to expend all of your energy fighting with contentious foes, that you can survive and transcend much of life's difficulty by allowing it to "be"; you don't have to take the bait and get into old, repetitive struggles that experience has taught you will only make things worse. *Just do it:* the old truism that you can't make an omelette without breaking an egg is a useful one. Take the plunge, say yes, do what you've always said you wanted to do. As we've seen, this doesn't mean you should capsize your life on a whim; it means you may take positive action that you know you can handle.

Remember what we explored about decision making and the kind of self-honesty it entails. How achievable do our Seven Goals for the Grown-up Woman seem now? Review the list: (1) To be self-supporting; (2) To be fulfilled on your own, with or without a mate; (3) To acknowledge that you are the major contributor to your own life — that you have consented to be who and where you are; (4) To seek people who respect and appreciate you; (5) To fulfill commitments to people who depend on you; (6) To be involved in "the family of man," to make the world a better place; and (7) To make peace with your past, to forgive yourself for making mistakes without dwelling on them, and to go forward with your life. Do these goals now make more sense to you, now that you've begun, imaginatively, to try them on for size?

Think back to our exploration of love in our chapters "With Him" and "Without Him." What does love mean from your new, self-reliant perspective? Remember our conclusion: that you're always "enough" no matter what your man status. And remember what we've said about bringing your *whole* self to work, learning from the example of women like Karen, who managed to achieve independence and self-sufficiency working with her husband; Anna, who learned to use her skills to better her position rather than complaining about what she couldn't change; and Monia and Bonnie, who have found ways to sustain their friendship *and* their working relationship. You always have the power to create a more satisfying work life for and by yourself, no matter what your present job circumstances may be.

What I hope you've learned above all is that you have abundant personal power to live the life you want to live. You have, and have always had, all the inner resources you've ever needed to direct yourself to real fulfillment. Growth, as you've seen, starts with seeing who and where you are *at this moment.* You can get your life moving anytime you want; you've exactly what it takes to move ahead right now. But before you make the first choices to get your life moving, it's a good idea to have a vision of where you want to go, what you ultimately want to achieve. What I'd like to leave you with now is something that will help you to unify your quest, put it in perspective, and help you to feel and achieve as much purpose in your life as possible. You now know something about the importance of self-definition and self-reliance; now it's time to decide what's important to you so that you can feel confident about putting that self-reliance to good use.

■ ■ ■ ■ ■ ■ ■ ■ ■ ■ ■ ■ ■ ■

Developing Your Own Philosophy

Deciding what is important to you is the greatest gift you can give yourself: it is what will give your life consistent direction and meaning. Developing a clear set of values and a basic philosophy of life that come from within you — not that you make the Feminine Mistake of acquiring from outside yourself — will help you to feel serenity

about facing critical decisions. Knowing what your true
best self would do in any situation can become your clearest, most trustworthy guide: it will help you to know
when to say yes and when to say no. Developing your
own philosophy means the difference between living a
life of inner peace and purpose and a life that is full of
difficult, wrenching decisions — decisions that wrench
because you're in constant conflict with yourself. This
isn't to say that any philosophy you come up with will
always be watertight, or that you won't suffer some confusion and regret about decisions you make. But you'll
suffer so much less if you give yourself the opportunity
to discover and live from your own values — what's really
important to you when the chips are down.

When you examine your own values, you commonly
come face-to-face with some of the most deeply rooted
outside voices you know. Remember, earlier on, when I
asked you to write some of the directions your internalized, other voices gave you and to attempt to replace them
with what *you* really believe and want for yourself? I
probably don't have to remind you how hard this was,
how difficult it can be to separate what you believe from
the received wisdom of others. But it's an essential task
if you want to increase a sense of peace with yourself.

Don't worry if you don't accomplish all of this "perfectly." Discovering your own values is an ongoing process, and your findings will change and evolve throughout
your life. That's why I headed this section with the word
developing: it implies something continuing. Deciding on
your values doesn't mean clinging to dogma out of fear.
While your quest may be to find a ruling principle, you
should never keep yourself from questioning what you
find; a part of your vigilance means staying vigilantly
receptive. To me, a true test of maturity is the ability to
admit you are wrong. When you truly listen — with your

heart and mind, and with the attitude that you can learn from what you hear — you may hear things that will encourage you to modify your course. The ability to accept criticism constructively is a priceless asset. If you go into an argument and, after carefully reflecting on what each side had to say, come out with a different opinion from the one you had when you went into it, you've discovered something very precious: you have proven to yourself that you're willing to change and grow. Congratulate yourself when you realize you were wrong. It means that you now realize more of the *truth* than you did before. You've permitted yourself to learn something.

You've already seen that it's only by learning to listen to yourself that you've got a chance to forge your own road to fulfillment — and a chance of happiness. And the goal of listening to yourself is perhaps primarily to discover what your own ethics are — your philosophy — so that you have something strong against which to measure the onslaught of advice others are only too willing to give you.

You've already started to find that philosophy in yourself simply by participating in this book, and you are finding a voice with more to tell you than any outside voice ever could. Change, as we've seen, has to start from within. Only when you've taken the necessary measures of weighing options and heeding your inner voice can change successfully manifest itself outside. Even as large a goal as changing our society has to start with changing ourselves individually. That's what you have the opportunity to do right now. And the need for positive change — not only in your own individual life, but in the dependent and enfeebled society we have allowed to grow around us — has become urgent.

Not long ago at a luncheon I attended, Ted Turner, head of CNN and founder of the Better World Society, said that our planet had perhaps fifteen years before we reached a point of no return in terms of the environmental destruction we human beings are causing. This poor planet, which, like each of our lives, offers so many gifts but is at the mercy of its inhabitants, needs to be healed. We see in the microcosm of our lives what we need to do in the macrocosm of society: individually and collectively we need to take stock, see what needs to be done, and then do it.

This observation isn't the departure from this book it may seem to be: it's really an extension of our choice-making theme. When we start to appreciate the impact we have on other people and that others have had on us — which is what we've been exploring here from page one — we can't help but see that we've got the same power to heal or wound, help or hamper, create or destroy in a larger, societal sense. As we've seen, happiness cannot develop in isolation, and a good deal of the responsibility entailed in becoming a grown-up human being, woman or man, means looking out for each other.

But you can't help others if you haven't first reached inside to help yourself. As urgent as it is to learn to make choices that will better the larger world, it's more urgent, first, to make choices that will help us to appreciate and utilize our own individual resources. Be prepared to make mistakes but also to welcome them. They're how we learn. And, believe me, I know — I've made them all! The Feminine Mistake can have a bewildering variety of manifestations, and the way it commonly manifested itself in women in the 1950s, 1960s, 1970s, and 1980s isn't in the least abstract to me. I lived out each one of them.

In the 1950s, my greatest fear was that I'd get my B.A. before my MRS. I never wore glasses on a date: it was more important to be pretty than to see. When I got married, I suffered terrible guilt about having to work to help support my family: I suffered every time anyone commented on the fact that my "real role" was as a mother, and how dare I leave my children in order to work. . . . In the 1960s, I "hated" men along with the best of them; I couldn't put them down fast or hard enough. I identified with what I thought was liberation but was really anger — anger that tied me to the past every bit as tightly as had my 1950s assumptions about being a wife and mother. I watched as wonderful mothers, friends of mine, got divorced and became promiscuous, following the call of the times that happiness could be found in "free love." I might have gone the divorce route too except that I couldn't tolerate the idea of doing to my children what my mother had done to me. . . . In the 1970s, my career became everything. I made excuses about why I had to work longer and harder than everyone else, but in the back of my mind I was desperately seeking approval and acceptance, hoping that perhaps if I were a success I could finally get my parents to love me. These struggles — and mistakes — have, however, led me in the past decade to a strong and rich sense of self. Making the mistakes I've made has taught me not only that I can survive to make new and better choices, but that I have the power to avoid those mistakes in the future. The prize is a deep sense of self-acceptance. I no longer feel the need to blame anyone, past or present, for any predicament in which I find myself. I've learned a simple truth: only I have power over my life, to change my life. The adventure and responsibility of exercising this power give my life meaning — more meaning than I ever dreamed I'd find when, as a young girl, I made the first tentative steps toward the "new me," with the help of my mentor, Leah.

You can achieve this self-acceptance and self-reliance, too. Achieving it is what will enable you truly to make a new life — to look forward, not backward. The best years of my life began in my forties, because that's when I made peace with myself. That's when I learned the truth of the Facts of Life we covered in chapter 2 — when I could let go of my anger, of the need to control; when I could let go of that sense of entitlement I grappled so bitterly with as a young girl and woman ("Why couldn't I have had more love, money, support, security . . . ?"). I now know that everything doesn't have to be a 10. A 7½ will do.

Nobody ever finishes with the evolutionary process I'm talking about. Beware of people who think they're a finished product. They have allowed something to die in them, no matter how impressive their outer selves may seem. Only when you allow yourself to be nurtured, cultivated, and fed can you grow and be happy. That nurturance and cultivation can go on until the last moment of life. If you welcome this process of growth, you'll be able to make the best statement about yourself I can imagine making: "I spent my life living — everything I truly wanted for myself I tried to achieve." People don't regret the things they did as much as they regret the things they didn't do. Our goal isn't merely to become aware of who we'd like to be, based on our own inner voices; it's to bring that hoped-for self into being.

It's helpful to have a reminder of this goal, something tangible you can hold in your hand.

■■■■■■■■■■■■■■■

Your Totem

When I read Jean Auel's *The Clan of the Cave Bear* I was so moved that I phoned her. I needed to tell her how much I loved — and identified with — her story of the primitive girl Ayla, who, thrust into a society that treated her as an outcast, nonetheless was able to find strength and purpose through the love and support of one member of that society who understood her, the medicine woman. Leah, whom I've told you about, was my medicine woman. But what especially struck me was the totem that the woman gave to Ayla. I couldn't believe it! I had already made a totem for myself, and it gave me the same hope and strength and comfort as Ayla's gave her. I'm not normally a superstitious person, but I never travel without this totem. What exactly is it?

It is a collection of charms on a gold chain. Each charm has a meaning. The first charm is a New York subway token, which reminds me of where I came from, what my life could have been like had I not taken the steps I took to change it. The second charm is an *S* for Sonya, a reminder to maintain my identity, to stick to what I know is right for me, to live my life according to my highest ethical standards. The third charm is a die that I got in Las Vegas, to remind me to be grateful for the good fortune I've had in my life, and that, the harder I work, the more good fortune I seem to enjoy. The fourth charm carries the words *Trust Me*, to remind me that most people who say "trust me" don't mean it, and that if I say it, I'd better mean it; it's a reminder that my word is bankable. The fifth charm is a hand of God, to remind me of the universal connectedness of things, of the sense of spirituality I've always felt in my life, and that every action I take has a consequence, every decision in my life has a ripple effect that joins me to the rest of humanity.

My totem has gotten me through many moments of confusion. It is a kind of lifeline to myself. I'm convinced that every woman should have a totem — a private reminder of your triumphs and your hardest lessons, a private message to yourself that you are worthy, you have faced and conquered fear, you are on your way to becoming a fulfilled human being. The lessons you are learning about self-reliance and inner direction are so important that they deserve some kind of tangible recognition, some actual object you can turn to when you start to doubt your ability to live self-reliantly, when the old messages threaten to take over again.

Make this kind of reminder for yourself. Mark your progress in a way that only you will understand. It doesn't have to be a charm bracelet or necklace. It might be a little notebook in which you write reminders you know you'll find healing when things get rough. It might be a little bag containing a few small objects that have meaning to you: a ticket stub from a play you went to see on your own, a paper clip from a report you made yourself do at work that you never thought you could complete. (If you've got that binder for a journal I recommended earlier on, you might make that the repository for these keepsakes, these "trophies.") Anything that has meaning to you can become this kind of resonant reminder to yourself about your own growth.

I promise that you'll grow to cherish your totem. You'll cherish it because of what you know it signifies: you've learned to cherish yourself. That's the most rewarding dividend that learning true self-reliance can bring you: an abiding, nurturing self-love. Please think of this book as a roadmap to that self-love, to valuing your most precious asset, one in which you can always invest and that will always grow in value: you. Once you start to value this asset as much as it deserves to be valued, you'll be on the way to creating the life you want for yourself. You'll have done something more: created real clarity in your life, a clarity that affords you a sharper view not only of who you are and what is really going on around you, but of who you could be, of what you might help the world around you to become. You'll have created that clear day in which you can truly see yourself.

You must create this clarity in order to have any hope of truly changing your life. I hope this book has helped you to do just that. But I hope you've discovered with me something equally important: moving toward fulfillment means adding value to your life. If you don't value your life — who you are and what you're capable of doing to become who you want to be — all you'll have are wishes and regrets. So, value the wonderful asset of yourself. Don't settle for less than you deserve.

Don't make a wish — make a life.

About the Author

A practicing psychologist and therapist, Dr. Sonya Friedman hosts her own daily television show on CNN, "Sonya Live," and writes a weekly column for the *Detroit Free Press*. She lives in New York City and suburban Detroit with her husband, Stephen.

Guy Kettelhack is the author or coauthor of numerous self-help books. He lives in New York City.